"As a Chaplain in the
needs of our Soldiers. I.
way of life whether at home or abroad, in combat or peace. Writing a devotional
based on his combat experiences in Iraq, Mike tells a story of courage, selfless
service, and faith skillfully linked to his experiences as a testimony of his personal
trials and tribulations."

- General Raymond T. Odierno, U.S. Army-
Ret. 38th Chief of Staff of The U.S. Army

"Mike's devotions speak to my heart and convey spiritual truth's that are easy
to understand. I'm not a military member, but these practical, reader-friendly
devotions are illustrated with stories that resonate with me and quickly pierce the
heart. I believe they would be an encouragement to anyone."

- Donnie Smith, President and CEO of Tyson Foods, Inc.

"A tremendous testament of heartfelt truth, motivation and a clear azimuth from
God's Blessings to overcome any challenge and excel!"

- General James Thurman, U.S. Army, Retired

"An inspiring collection of personal combat experiences and devotional thoughts
from the heart of a humble servant of God who has spent most of his vocational
ministry "bringing Soldiers to God and God to Soldiers." Chaplain Colonel Mike
Tarvin's compelling stories, each woven around a specific biblical truth, will lead
the reader to conclude that the Word of God is practical, relevant, and timeless for
all the seasons of our lives, regardless of one's stature, environment, or situation. A
must read for those needing a daily dose of encouraging wisdom."

- Doug Carver, Chaplain (Major General) USA-Ret. 22nd Chief
of Chaplains (2007-2011), United States Army Executive Director
of the Chaplaincy, North American Mission Board, SBC

"We met Mike Tarvin when Third Day toured in Iraq. From the get-go I could
see that he was a fine leader of people and a great follower of Jesus. His care for
folks and his love for the Lord come across strongly in these devotions."

- Mac Powell, Lead Singer for Third Day (Third Day is a
Christian rock band that has earned four GRAMMYs (11
nominations) and 24 GMA Dove Awards (42 nominations)

---

* The views presented here are my own and do not necessarily represent
the views of the Department of Defense or its Components.

"Strong. Powerful. Challenging. Relevant. Regardless of your vocation or whatever you may be going through in your life, these devotionals will empower you to live your life in the highest manner, realizing all God has for you today."
    - Dr. Ronnie Floyd, President, Southern Baptist Convention, Senior Pastor, Cross Church

"Mike's words make evident that Scripture is practical, life-giving, and applicable to every situation. His insight comes from one who has lived in the trenches with his parishioners. In these pages you will find a daily dose of courage!"
    - Brenda Pace, author, teacher and motivational speaker

"When I read these devotions and how powerful they are I think of my Soldiers and how they may help them as it helps me. I would encourage anyone to read these inspiring devotions for comfort and encouragement. Mike does it best!"
    - Ronald T. Riling, Command Sergeant Major (CSM), U.S. Army, Retired – (CSM Riling, was awarded the Silver Star for conspicuous gallantry in action while serving with the 1ˢᵗ Brigade Combat Team, 1ˢᵗ Infantry Division, during combat operations for Operation IRAQI FREEDOM)

"The thing I like about these devotions is that they provide practical, reader-friendly lessons. They get into your heart. A book of great inspiration, courage, and hope; every word rings with reflection, truth, kindness, and the beauty of the human spirit. I urge you to check out this book."
    - Alvin Jay Chaplin Sr., Sergeant Major, US Army

"The apostle Paul tells us that followers of Jesus can learn much from the life of a soldier. Mike Tarvin uses his military experience to offer up a plentiful supply of genuine insight and Godly wisdom for the believer's daily journey and spiritual battle."
    - Rev. Nigel James, tour pastor, Third Day.

"An inspiring read that provides excellent tidbits of spiritual motivation from one of God's faithful servants."
    - Stephen A. Stott, Sergeant Major, U.S. Army, Retired

---

*   The views presented here are my own and do not necessarily represent the views of the Department of Defense or its Components.

Lamar & Dixie, old and special friends. I pray this book will cause each of you to shine as an even brighter:

LIGHT IN THE MIDST OF DARKNESS

(Devotions From Combat)

Lamar while we were in Iraq you were part of the Light in that often dark place that kept me focused. Thanks my friend. Love you both! Blessings, Mike

Michael D. Tarvin

WESTBOW
PRESS®
A DIVISION OF THOMAS NELSON
& ZONDERVAN

The light shines in the darkness, and the darkness has not overcome it.

John 1:5

This book is a work of non-fiction. Unless otherwise noted, the author
and the publisher make no explicit guarantees as to the accuracy of
the information contained in this book and in some cases, names of
people and places have been altered to protect their privacy.

WestBow Press books may be ordered through booksellers or by contacting:

WestBow Press
A Division of Thomas Nelson & Zondervan
1663 Liberty Drive
Bloomington, IN 47403
www.westbowpress.com
1 (866) 928-1240

Because of the dynamic nature of the Internet, any web addresses or
links contained in this book may have changed since publication and
may no longer be valid. The views expressed in this work are solely those
of the author and do not necessarily reflect the views of the publisher,
and the publisher hereby disclaims any responsibility for them.

Any people depicted in stock imagery provided by Thinkstock are models,
and such images are being used for illustrative purposes only.
Certain stock imagery © Thinkstock.

ISBN: 978-1-5127-3302-0 (sc)
ISBN: 978-1-5127-3303-7 (hc)
ISBN: 978-1-5127-3301-3 (e)

Library of Congress Control Number: 2016903427

Print information available on the last page.

WestBow Press rev. date: 04/25/2016

INTRODUCTION

"Light In The Midst of Darkness" did not start out as a book project. I was doing a tour in Iraq as the Command Chaplain for Multi-National Corps-Iraq (senior chaplain for all operational units in Iraq). Our Commanding General was Lieutenant General Raymond Odierno who would later get his fourth star and become the Chief of Staff of the Army (senior leader in the Army).

I was determined not to let the fast pace, long hours, countless attacks and deaths drag me down physically, emotionally, mentally or spiritually. So as part of my routine I made sure that I was up extra early each morning for a run or exercise and that was followed by my own personal Bible study and prayer. I began to record some devotional type writings and those have now been re-written by me as actual devotionals.

The devotions in this book are not just for Soldiers, Marines, Airmen or Sailors. They come from the experiences of the great men and women who wore those uniforms, but the lessons and insights are for anyone who wants to deepen their experience with God and increase their spiritual life in a very real way.

This is the perfect book for those who want to enhance their walk with God. The devotions are easy to read, short and applicable to life. It does not matter if you are a business person, a farmer, teacher, student, pastor, public servant, mother, father, daughter or son, this book will speak to your life and to your spirit. It is **perfect for individual study or for use by a family, women or men's groups, Sunday school classes, couples or Bible studies.** I pray that you will be blessed through your reading of this devotional book.

DEDICATION

I dedicate this book to my family.

My first dedication is to my Mom, who bravely battled Alzheimer's and is waiting in heaven for my Dad and the rest of us to join her. She was a constant supporter in my life. As a young boy, she allowed me to live life, to feel safe and cared for 24/7. She and my Dad made it to every baseball game, every concert, every play, and every cross-country or track meet. I could always hear my Mom cheering for me. She believed in me. **Thanks Mom, I love you!**

Dad, both you and Grandpa showed me what a real man of hard-work and integrity is all about. You, like Mom, came to all those events. I now know that took a great effort and extra hours at work. You and Mom created a home that enabled all three of your children to be loving, caring, and successful. **Thanks Dad, I love you!**

Rachel and Rebekah, my two wonderful daughters, each of you in your own way has brought me more joy than I ever imagined. Never have I felt more blessed than when I first beheld you as newborns and heard those sweet cries. You are each beautiful young women who still bring me great joy and happiness. **Thanks Rachel and Rebekah, I love you!**

Amy, my wife and friend, my last dedication is to you. "Saving the best for last" is true in this case. I can't even hope to capture in words what you mean to me. Every day I thank God for your presence in my life. That first time I saw you I was smitten. Today, I love you even more than the day we said, "I do." You have been a faithful, loving, kind, compassionate, wife. You are an intelligent and talented woman who tirelessly gives of herself to others; most especially to me. I've learned about giving because of you. I want to be better because of you and I am better because of you. **Thanks Amy, I love you!**

This Book is
IN MEMORY OF

U.S. Army Chaplain (CPT) Dale Goetz and Staff Sergeant Christopher Todd Stout. Chaplain Dale Goetz was assigned to 1st Battalion, 66th Armor Regiment, 1st Brigade Combat Team, 4th Infantry Division. Dale was Killed in Action in the Arghandab River Valley in Afghanistan. Staff Sergeant Stout was a Chaplain Assistant for the 1-508 Parachute Infantry Regiment, 82nd Airborne Division, Killed in Action while repelling an insurgent attack in Kandahar City, Afghanistan.
Dale and Chris were two of the most faithful and devoted men of God to serve our nation.

I have come into the world as a light,
so that no one who believes in me
should stay in darkness.
John 12:46

ACKNOWLEDGMENTS

This is the most risky aspect of the book. How do I acknowledge those who have helped shape me? First, I ask for forgiveness. I know someone will read this and think, "Why did he not write my name down?" I'm sorry. I realize that who and what I am is due to many others who have been a part of my life.

First, I thank God. I don't know where I'd be or what I'd be doing today without Jesus in my life. Literally, my relationship with God, through Jesus Christ, turned my life around.

I already wrote a dedication to my wife and daughters, but I have to acknowledge their support here as well. The Army is a tough life and I don't know how many birthdays, holidays and other special events I missed, I don't even want to count. There were over 20 moves and so many different schools and church homes that made it hard to put down deep roots. Yet, through it all, you were there. Sometimes willingly and sometimes not, but you were always there. That also includes my extended family. My parents, brother and sister, grandparents, in-laws, all of you stood by my side and I'm grateful.

Thanks to the friends who led me to Christ and helped mentor me. Some of them include: Lynn Lavery, Brad and Cid Beyer, Jerry and Debbie Rittenhouse, Roger and Gail McKinney, and Paul and Peg Lintern.

All the Soldiers I've served with over the years have been great. My first assignment was in Germany at a little caserne named Turley Barracks. There I worked and lived with a group of Officers and NCOs that would shape my life. My first platoon sergeant was Howard Rathman. How grateful I am that I allowed myself to be trained by him, and to learn from him. My fellow LTs, Sulka, Tessino, Caniglia, Schroeder, and Lawless all kept me sane and were the best of friends. I also worked with Teen Challenge in Germany and learned about ministry and leadership from Howard Foltz, Clive Beckham, Al Perna, Carolyn Hedgpeth, Lynne Anne Martin, Kim Hancock, Tom Rennard, Kevin and Eunice and others.

As a chaplain in the military, I had so many other chaplains that I was honored to work with and count as friends. I started out as a chaplain with people like Ken Yates, Barry White, Randy Heckert, Dave Peterson, Darrell Thomsen, Matt Goff, Tom Solhjem, Steve Berry, Michael Coffey, Will Parker, Hal Roller and Karen Diefendorf. I worked with others like Dave Waters, Lamar Griffin, Will Laigaie, Ron Thomas, Jim White, Mike Thompson, Mike Hoyt, Ken Stice, Bobby Whitlock, Dave Smartt, Eric Albertson, Sonny Moore, Dave Curlin, Jeff Streuker, Bill Harrison, Steve Peck, John Manuel, Mike Klein, Kerry Steedley, Ray Bailey, Oscar Arauco, Dan Stallard, Dave Mansberger, Shon Neyland, Michael Langston, Kim Norwood, Bob Phillips, Barb Sherer, Sam Boone, Sherrill Munn, Paul Hurley, Bob Land, Jim Agnew, Ron Casteel, Mark Roeder, John Cook, Sherman Baker, Bill Nesbit, Brad Fipps, Warren Haggray, Ken Hurst, Bob Wichman, and a host of others.

I've been blessed to serve with some of the very best leaders in Army, starting with the former Chief of Staff of the Army, General Raymond T. Odierno. Others include Generals James D. Thurman, Charles (Hondo) Campbell, John Campbell and Vincent Brooks; Lieutenant Generals George Crocker, Eric Schoomaker, Joseph Anderson, Patricia Horoho, Joseph Peterson, Thomas Turner, John Wood, Daniel Bolger and Howard Bromberg; and Major Generals Gary Volesky, Dana Pittard, Doug Carver, Don Rutherford, Jerry Haberek and Bob Dees. I also served with LTC Ken Stauss, the best of the best, a true RANGER who died serving our country.

I served with some amazing NCOs: CSMs, Howard Rathman, Ron Riling, Neil Ciotola, Dennis Carey and Phillip Kiniery. I was also honored to stand shoulder to shoulder with Chaplain Assistant NCOs such as SGMs Alvin Chaplin, Chantel Sena-Diaz, Tyronne Wright, Steve Stott and Gary Oulette; MSGs Deborah Carter and George Johnson, SSGs Chris Solorio, Denise Monroe, Jason Robinson and a host of other NCOs who make the Army run day in and day out.

Thanks to Bonnie Sizemore and Melissa Brannan. Bonnie edited the devotions and was a great help and a blessing. Melissa also helped me with editing and polishing my wording. Thank you Bonnie and Melissa, for making this a better book.

Once again, I know I missed someone important. I'm sorry. The point is, this book has been a team effort and I had a ton of stellar teammates. Thank you! If you were one of those who helped me along the way and I did not mention you, "Thank You" even more.

My use of Scripture is from the New International Version and I am grateful to publishers of the New International Version of the Bible for granting permission for its use. THE HOLY BIBLE, NEW INTERNATIONAL VERSION®, NIV® Copyright © 1973, 1978, 1984, 2011 by Biblica, Inc.® Used by permission. All rights reserved worldwide.

A note to all you grammar hounds; I intentionally capitalize the word Soldier when used to refer to our U.S. or allied Soldiers. The same way with Airmen, Sailor, and Marine. I did not capitalize satan or the devil (you gotta earn that capital).

Finally, be strong in the Lord and in his mighty power.
Put on the full armor of God so that you can
take your stand against the devil's schemes.
Ephesians 6: 10-11

Today was my first day in the combat area of operations. After a one night stay at Camp Buehring in Kuwait, we flew to Iraq. The first part of our journey, from Texas to Kuwait, was on a big commercial jet, where we had stewardesses, snacks, movies and cokes. It was a long trip from Fort Hood, Texas to Kuwait but a pretty good experience overall.

Today's flight to Iraq brought the reality of war a little closer to home. We flew to Baghdad, Iraq on a C-130 military plane and had to wear our helmets and protective vests. For the last thirty-five miles or so, the pilots flew Nap of the Earth. Nap of the Earth means flying low and fast with lots of jerking around and following the contours of the earth to avoid possible enemy fire and radar. Our getting fully geared up for entry into the war zone reminded me of Ephesians 6: 10-18, which tells us to put on the full armor of God. Soldiers are called to be prepared to go into battle. Likewise, Christians are called to be prepared to face the rigors of everyday life, which is a battle of its own, with a very real enemy who has a goal of defeating you.

I encourage you to take seriously the mandate to put on God's armor of truthfulness, righteousness, (readiness that comes from the Gospel of Peace), faithfulness, salvation, and God's Word. I will write more about this armor later in this devotional book. Commit yourself to be ready to live for God and to let God's light shine in your life.

Take the helmet of salvation and the sword of the Spirit,
which is the word of God.
Ephesians 6: 17

Yesterday, I wrote about God's armor and the last part of that armor is God's Word. The door of my "hootch" (the term for our quarters) where I sleep has a sign on the inside. The same sign is posted in every hootch and provides guidance for all Soldiers. It is entitled, "React to Indirect Fire," (mortars and rockets shot by the enemy) and tells us what to do during an attack. I read through those directions very carefully, because like most Soldiers who are in Afghanistan and Iraq I was interested in living through an attack. I did not want to die. I had a pretty good idea of what to do, but I wanted to make sure I had not overlooked some action that might make a difference to my survival.

Amazingly, we have a similar document that allows us to survive this life and eventually enter into eternity with God. While the consequences of failing to follow the directions of the "React to Indirect Fire" sign are dire, they are not nearly as devastating as failing to follow the guidance, direction, and wisdom of the Bible. Survival in a battle zone is important, but survival in life and eternity far outweighs that aspect of life. God has graciously given us His Word to help us in our quest for surviving and even excelling in the communities in which we live.

Today is a good day to commit or re-commit to following the ultimate guidance of God's directions in your life. Make that commitment, and you will begin to know real security in the midst of life's challenges and the enemy's "indirect fire."

Your Word is a Lamp to my feet and light on my path.
Psalm 119:105

The sign that I wrote about yesterday is not the only message posted on the inside of the door where I live. Another one of the signs in my hootch says, "**<u>Always</u>** keep outside porch light off." I'm not sure why they built the living areas for our Soldiers with these lights in the first place. The contractor probably had a design which was followed despite the danger the lights might create. No one caught it until it was too late. The reason for the "no porch light" policy is to prevent the lights from providing a steady, constant target point for the enemy. It is a good idea, but it makes it very dark, especially during this winter season. At this time of the year, when Soldiers wake up, go to work, and when they come back from work, it is almost pitch black. So you often need the benefit of a flashlight. Every Soldier at Camp Victory carries some sort of light to find his or her way and to prevent falling in a hole, ditch, or some other unseen hazard. It only takes one tumble into a ditch for that lesson to be learned.

That same concept works for us with God's Word. Psalm 119:105 says, "Your Word is a lamp to my feet and a light for my path." Reading and studying God's Word, the Bible, will help you avoid many of life's hazards. When you do encounter life's hazards and challenges, God's Word will help you overcome them. With God's light you will find that the risks and perils of life are much easier to survive and positively resolve. We all need direction in our life, and God's Word is the ultimate source of positive direction. Are you making sure you have a steady source of light in this dark world? Look to God's Word for your light in the midst of darkness.

But when he, the Spirit of truth, comes, he will guide you into all the truth. He will not speak on his own; he will speak only what he hears, and he will tell you what is yet to come.
John 16:13

I woke up at 2:54 a.m. I'm not sure if it was because of jet lag (plus being half way around the world and my body clock not recognizing it was supposed to be asleep) or if I heard the sound of an explosion. However, I am certain that right after I woke up, I heard two explosions at an unknown distance away. It sounded loud and maybe it was close, but it also seemed somewhat far away (if that makes sense). After lying there for a few minutes, it became clear that was all there was to the enemy's attack. I later learned a piece of equipment was destroyed, but no persons were hurt and the explosion turned out to be about a quarter of a mile from my location. As I reflected on this, I think I probably heard something. Although it was not a conscious act, my mind subconsciously reacted.

God, through the Holy Spirit, does the same thing if we are sensitive to the Spirit's leading. It may not be that you are awakened from sleep; but you will notice or feel when something is not right or when you are being urged to act. My experience is that we often fail to heed that prodding. Consequently, we miss out on a blessing or we experience a bad result we could have avoided. Many times we ignore God's direction because we are worried about what others will think of us if we are too "holy" or follow God too intently in our day-to-day life.

Don't fall into that trap. If we are sensitive to God, we can often avoid problems or danger. We may even enjoy a blessing by following the guidance of God. More important than the avoidance of trouble or the receipt of a blessing, we need to focus on walking obediently with God. The closer we walk to God, the more likely we are to circumvent the pit-falls of life.

Be alert and of sober mind. Your enemy the devil
prowls around like a roaring lion looking for someone to devour.
1 Peter 5:8

Tomorrow, I am scheduled to go visit some Religious Support Teams (RSTs) in the southeast portion of Baghdad. For this trip, I will travel by ground convoy through some dangerous areas. A few friends, who have been here for a while, gave me some advice.

One friend said to make sure I stayed alert at all times and that whatever happened not to panic. He reminded me of the good training I'd received on how to act and react. Another friend said much the same thing, but he focused on telling me to make sure to watch everyone around me. He said that the insurgents are out looking for opportunities to create chaos and terror. Basically, he was telling me to be alert for danger.

Again I'm drawn to the similarity of our spiritual life. The verse in 1 Peter 5:8 calls for the believer to be alert and sober. Another version uses the word *self-controlled* in place of *sober*. We are called to be alert and self-controlled because the enemy, the devil, prowls around like a roaring lion looking for someone to devour.

Just like the insurgents and the terrorists want to defeat freedom and justice; the devil is out to destroy the Christian. Part of God's direction to us for dealing with this danger is found in this verse. The same principles work for us and the demons we face every day.

Christian, are you self-controlled, or do you "lose it" too easily? If your language or actions are out of control, the enemy has been successful in his attacks. Be on the alert; stay aware of your situation. The desire of the enemy is simple and harsh. He wants to destroy you. Staying alert and self-controlled helps the believer avoid or react responsibly to challenges and attacks in life.

I lift up my eyes to the hills where does my help come from?
My help comes from the Lord, the Maker of heaven and earth.
Psalm 121:1-2

As usual, I was up early today but I did not do my normal physical fitness training this morning. Instead, I went to the dining facility and had breakfast with my Sergeant Major, the Military Police (MP) Chaplain, and his Chaplain Assistant. After breakfast, we went over to the MP headquarters and then down to the motor pool for a convoy safety brief. The Sergeant Major and I were traveling by ground convoy with the MP Chaplain and some other Military Police Soldiers to a Forward Operating Base in the southeast portion of Baghdad.

Although none of the great Soldiers who were part of the convoy were overtly fearful; their anxiety was palpable. The route we were taking was through the International Zone and some other key areas of Baghdad that are often areas of sniper fire and vehicle borne improvised explosive device (IED) attacks. Many of the Soldiers with me had been on this route before and knew the danger.

After the final check on our radios, where all the vehicle leaders signaled their readiness to move out and begin the mission, everyone who desired to participate was comforted and encouraged as we paused to pray over the radio.

The verse for today comes from a time when religious pilgrims heading to Jerusalem were on a dangerous route, and they called on God for help. Today you can do the same: look to God for help as you travel your own difficult path, whatever it may be.

Put on the full armor of God
so that you can take your stand against the devil's schemes.
Ephesians 6:11

Yesterday's purposeful trip through "bad-guy" territory made me grateful for all the protection I had. My High Mobility Multipurpose Wheeled Vehicle (Humvee) had extra armor installed to help protect against bomb blasts and bullets. Each of the three Soldiers on board had a personal weapon, and there was a 50 caliber machine gun on top of the vehicle with a gunner manning it.

Additionally, the vehicle had a special attachment added to the front designed to cause certain types of improvised explosive devices (IEDs) to detonate prior to the vehicle getting to the IED. We also had special windows that had been added to the Humvee, designed to reduce the effects from bombs exploding and sniper or small arms fire.

The last addition to the vehicle was a protective cupola that went around the rotating 50 Caliber machine gun. This not only helps protect the gunner, but also allows him to rotate his machine gun quickly toward the area of likely risk or respond to actual enemy fire and return fire efficiently.

Personally, all of us wore helmets on our heads, with protective goggles or glasses for our eyes. We had on body armor with special breast, back and side plates and also add-on armor for the shoulders and upper arms. There was even an armored groin protector, along with our normal uniforms and boots.

Spiritually, God calls all of us to put on His armor to protect us and to help us fight back against the enemy. As well protected as I was on my trip through dangerous territory, God's armor is even more effective while on our spiritual journey.

Take a few minutes to review the devotions you read during this past week. Write down three key lessons you learned. What aspect of the week's devotions resonates most with you? (If you are participating as a group or family take time to discuss these key lessons.)

_____

_____

_____

_____

Were there any aspects of the devotions that you had trouble identifying with? (If you are participating as a group or family take time to discuss the troubling portions.)

_____

_____

_____

_____

Write down names of people you know who might be struggling with some of the points from the devotions. Take time to pray for each person. (If you are participating as a group, or family take time to pray for the people identified.)

_____

_____

_____

_____

What changes do you feel God is calling you to make after reading last week's devotions? (If you are participating as a group or family take time to discuss those desired changes.)

_____

_____

_____

_____

Think about a personal example in your life that demonstrates the truth of the devotions. (If you are participating as a group or family take time to share some of the stories with each other.)

_____

_____

_____

_____

He tends his flock like a shepherd: He gathers the lambs in his arms
and carries them close to his heart; he gently l
eads those that have young.
Isaiah 40:11

The day started out as normal; I woke up around 4:45 a.m. and went to the gym. The maintenance of a fitness routine is essential at all times but even more so here, where one must remain strong and healthy. After breakfast I went to my office, which is currently right behind the dining facility. Later, I went over to the Victory Base Chapel where the chaplains assigned to medical units across Iraq were gathered for a short training conference. These specially trained chaplains do great work in caring for our wounded Soldiers and the medical staff of their units.

Just after lunch I was standing in a doorway with SGT Solorio when we heard a deafening explosion. The concussion knocked pictures off the wall and caused us to hit the floor and then find shelter. A total of seven 122 millimeter rockets hit our encampment and our neighbors at Camp Liberty. The cost was 14 Wounded in Action (WIA) and one Killed in Action (KIA). This was not an unexpected event as mortar and rocket fire are fairly regular, day-to-day occurrences. However, the attacks are also regularly inaccurate and previously had not been very effective.

This event reminded me of our need to be ready spiritually. Just as there are no safe areas here in Iraq, the same is true for all of this earthly life. Our only safe place is in the arms of God. Make sure you are ready and that you stay ready. Allow yourself to be part of God's flock and to be close to God's heart.

He will be a joy and delight to you,
and many will rejoice because of his birth.
Luke 1:14

What an unusual place this war zone can be. Yesterday was a day of attacks, reminding us of the danger and risk we face. Today was a complete change of pace with a live show for our Soldiers. The World Wrestling Association had a large group of men and women here to entertain our Soldiers. It was quite an extravaganza. The CEO and great former wrestler Vince McMahon was present, along with the Grave Digger, John Cena (who is the current "World Champion") and a bunch of other wrestlers, including some beautiful women wrestlers. The whole event will be televised in the U.S. for a big Christmas spectacular.

When the show started, there were hundreds of Soldiers, Sailors, Airmen and Marines surrounding the ring. I was amazed at how excited and fired up so many people were over this wrestling show. I understand many of the reasons for that fervor. I have to admit that it was fun to watch for a few minutes, but then I returned to my office to do some work.

I don't think it is realistic to expect Christians to show the same type of excitement in their faith expression as a wrestling fan at a match or football fans at a game. The venues are two totally different things. However, we would do well to understand that God does want us to appropriately exhibit our joy and excitement that is found in a relationship with God. If we have a lack of joy or excitement, it is a good sign we have a problem. We are called to Rejoice! We should be excited about what God has done and is doing with us. It should cause us to praise God.

It was not through law that Abraham and his offspring received the promise that he would be heir of the world, but through the righteousness that comes by faith.

Romans 4:13

Today is Sunday and, to be honest, Sundays at war in Iraq are not too much different than any other day, at least on the surface. We still get up early in the morning, attend briefings, working groups, and other meetings that occur as on any other day. Then of course, our Soldiers, Sailors, Airmen and Marines still end up fighting and sometimes dying or getting wounded.

There are no days off here in Iraq; however, Sundays seem to bring a slightly different attitude in most of the staff. Rest and worship have to be defined in new terms, but the concept is the same as back home. We offer a number of services throughout the day. We even do a "mini" Protestant and Catholic service in the Joint Operations Center where folks monitor and react to the battle on a 24 hour-a-day rotation. One of our services at the Victory Chapel is a traditional type Protestant service that begins at 0700 (7:00 a.m.). This morning, the Secretary of Defense (SECDEF), who is visiting Iraq, attended our service and I was the preacher. As you might guess, the presence of the SECDEF brings some unusual additions to the normal operations. For instance, last night, security officers came and searched the chapel for possible security risks.

What I had not planned on, was my experience as I arrived at the chapel this morning. There were security personnel and MPs at every door. In order to get into the chapel, we had to show our Multi-National Corp-Iraq ID badges. Yielding to security checks to enter church was a first for me. It made me think how grateful I am that God does not require anything other than our desire to come to Him. Just as God promised to Abraham, He receives all who come by faith. God will receive you just as you are, with no conditions.

Then one of the elders said to me, "Do not weep! See, the Lion of the tribe of Judah, the Root of David, has triumphed. He is able to open the scroll and its seven seals."

Revelation 5:5

The unit, which I'm assigned to in Iraq is the III Armored Corps from Fort Hood. It is realistic to say that it is the most powerful Army Corps in the world and has a long, proud history. Here in Iraq, the III Corps actually takes on the title of another unit called the Multi-National Corps-Iraq (MNC-I). We are composed of different units from the U.S., like the 1st Cavalry Division, the 25th Infantry Division, the II Marine Expeditionary Force, and portions of many other units (including a Parachute Infantry Brigade from the 82d Airborne Division and an infantry brigade from the 10th Mountain Division). We have a large support force comprised of multiple units; such as, the 13th Sustainment Command (Expeditionary), and the 3rd Signal Brigade. We also have great coalition partners and units from Britain, Korea, Poland, Australia, New Zealand, Macedonia, Georgia, and many other countries. The unification of all these forces represents an awesome amount of power. The patch we wear on our uniform to represent our unit (MNC-I), has the image of a large lion in the center. The lion's mouth is open in a roar and the lion is depicted as moving forward." This image is used to convey the power and authority of MNC-I.

An even greater power has also been portrayed as a lion: Jesus Christ. We often fail to realize the power and authority we have in Jesus Christ. As Christians we don't wear patches on our shoulder to indicate our "unit" affiliation; but if we did, one of the elements of our insignia could rightfully be the image of a strong, authoritative lion. I want to encourage you to live confidently, secure in the knowledge that Jesus makes us strong and mighty like a lion.

Jesus answered, "I am the way and the truth and the life.
No one comes to the Father except through me."
John 14:6

Yesterday, I wrote about our Lord as a strong and mighty lion, but that is not the only role of Jesus or of us as God's children. At one point in the Scripture above, Jesus says, "I am the way." I was recently talking to a Soldier at the Corps Headquarters, and he told me he was a new Christian. As we talked about his new life and what he was doing to grow as a believer, he said, "I just want to move forward; I don't want to regress." I suppose that is the desire of most of us; to move forward in our relationship with God and not fall back into old habits. We can easily get off track and find ourselves heading in the wrong direction.

The lion is not the only image on the Multi-National Corps-Iraq patch I described in yesterday's devotion. There is also a spear that runs vertically in the center of the patch. Among other things, it represents the concept of being at "the tip of the spear." The vertical spear indicates that the unit is up front, leading the way, and saying to all others, "Follow me, I'm moving forward, this is the way to go."

Jesus does the same thing. He is up front and leads the way, not just by words but also by his actions. Additionally, He tells us that not only can He show us the way but He actually is the way. What we do and say is important, but the most critical thing we can do to ensure we are on track is put our life in the hands of Jesus. Deciding to accept Jesus as Lord and Savior is the most important thing any of us will ever do. Continually trying to follow His lead is the surest way of moving forward in our lives.

And when the Israelites saw the mighty hand of the Lord displayed against the Egyptians, the people feared the Lord and put their trust in him and in Moses his servant.
Exodus 14:31

Today was a key day for our unit in Iraq. Our first two weeks "in country" were a transition period. Even though we have been doing our respective jobs for at least a week; today marked the official transition of authority from V Corps to III Corps. There was a large ceremony conducted to demonstrate the transfer.

The main element of a transition of authority or a change of command ceremony is not the speech of the senior general in country, but instead is the passing of the unit colors. This part of the ceremony includes both the outgoing and incoming Commanding Generals (CG) and their Command Sergeants Major (CSM). The flag that represents the command of Multi-National Corps-Iraq is passed from the outgoing CSM to his CG. That CG passes the flag to the CG of the higher command who in turn passes it to the incoming CG. Finally, the new Commanding General gives the Unit Colors (flag) to his CSM for safe keeping. The traditional passing of the flag signifies that authority for the command has been shifted to a new commander.

We, as servants of God, must do the same thing. When we realize we are called to be in a relationship with God, we accept Jesus Christ as Lord and Savior, and transfer authority of our lives to Him. We often demonstrate this transfer through baptism. Just as during the ceremony, where flags are passed, baptism signifies that authority for our command has shifted to Jesus.

Who has the authority in your life? Only God can safely see you to the end. You can't truly succeed or find fulfillment on your own. Trust God. Transition the authority from your own limited and flawed ability to God, the One of unlimited and flawless ability.

Do not let your hearts be troubled.
You believe in God; believe also in me.
John 14:1

Yesterday, our office helped conduct a special event at our primary headquarters located in the El-Faw Palace. As the seasons of Christmas and Hanukah were both upon us, we had a small ceremony in the rotunda of the palace to light a Christmas tree and the first candle on the Menorah. At the same time, Bill O'Reilly, the host of the Fox news show *The O'Reilly Factor*, was present in the palace, signing his new book and visiting our Soldiers. Mr. O'Reilly touts his show as the "No Spin Zone." Primarily this "no spin zone" moniker is used to indicate that only the unvarnished truth is presented, not opinions or subjective views.

As part of our Christmas tree lighting, we had one of our generals give a command to the youngest Soldier of MNC-I to, "Light the tree." We also invited Mr. O'Reilly to join the Soldier in pushing the button to light the tree. It was especially thrilling for the Soldier; and was also enjoyed by Mr. O'Reilly and the other Soldiers in attendance. There is something electrifying and enticing about the presence of celebrities that causes people to try and be near them. Mr. O'Reilly was gracious and kind, spending hours with our Soldiers, taking pictures and signing autographs.

Someday, we will find ourselves in the presence of God. Now that will be the true "No Spin Zone." For Christians, it will be a thrilling day. For those who don't have a personal relationship with Jesus, the day will be a sad and tragic time. Make sure you are in the first category; put your belief and trust in Jesus.

Take a few minutes to review the devotions you read during this past week. Write down three key lessons you learned. What aspect of the week's devotions resonates most with you? (If you are participating as a group or family take time to discuss these key lessons.)

_____

_____

_____

_____

Were there any aspects of the devotions that you had trouble identifying with? (If you are participating as a group or family take time to discuss the troubling portions.)

_____

_____

_____

_____

Write down names of people you know who might be struggling with some of the points from the devotions. Take time to pray for each person. (If you are participating as a group, or family take time to pray for the people identified.)

_____

_____

_____

_____

What changes do you feel God is calling you to make after reading last week's devotions? (If you are participating as a group or family take time to discuss those desired changes.)

_____

_____

_____

_____

Think about a personal example in your life that demonstrates the truth of the devotions. (If you are participating as a group or family take time to share some of the stories with each other.)

_____

_____

_____

_____

Then Jesus told his disciples a parable to show them that
they should always pray and not give up.
Luke 18:1 -

Before I left Fort Hood, Texas, and the United States to head for Iraq, my family celebrated an early Christmas because we knew I'd be gone in December. As part of our celebration, we exchanged gifts with each other. One gift from my wife was a small battery-operated light. It was yellow and had a smiley face on it that I could simply push to activate the light. My sweet wife told me to place it near my bed. That way I could not only have a light, but when I clicked it on, it would remind me of her. It seems silly; but this inexpensive, funny little light is such a comfort. Not only do I enjoy the light when I wake up in the pitch blackness, but I also am reminded of my wife and family when it comes on. In addition, I use that reminder to take a moment and thank God for my wife and to say a quick prayer for her and my two girls.

Prayer is important and valuable for everyone involved. I encourage you to put reminders in place that will help you pray. Place pictures in key places, or perhaps find an object to carry in your pocket or purse that will remind you to pray. Keep a prayer list in a notebook or an electronic device. The important thing is that you *pray*.

I take great comfort in the knowledge that many different people are praying for me. I'm convinced those prayers make a very real difference. Amazingly, the benefit of prayer is experienced by both the person being prayed for and the person praying. Be a person of prayer... and don't give up.

He will reply, "I tell you the truth,
whatever you did not do for one of the least of these,
you did not do for me."
Matthew 25:45

Information is a powerful thing, especially during combat operations. It can shape your actions for good or bad. Properly assessed information can help save lives. Therefore, we spend a good amount of time passing and assessing information. We do this in Battle Update Assessments and Battle Update Briefs. Quite honestly, sometimes it seems as if the majority of information is negative: numbers of coalition military killed in action and wounded in action, numbers and locations of improvised explosive devices (IEDs), local nationals murdered, reports of sectarian violence, and other similar accounts.

So, it is indeed a pleasure to find an opportunity to focus on positive news or events. Yesterday a group of us took donations of children's gifts, basic hygiene supplies, and simple non-prescription medical items to a Civil Military Operations Center (CMOC). The CMOC attempts to reach out to the local community in numerous ways and coordinates actions to assist the community. This particular CMOC is right next to an Iraqi community in Baghdad and runs a small medical clinic that provides care to needy families. The place is packed with children who are desperate for help, which they get at the CMOC in the form of medicine, medical treatment, clothing, food, and even small business-type loans for the adults.

It was good to see smiling children as they received needed clothes, medical care, food, and some toys and sports equipment to play with on the playground. Are you doing something to help "the least of these?" You should be. In a world where we constantly hear negative information, we can let it lead our perspective towards a sense of futility or we can act to create a positive outcome. Decide today to help someone in need.

"For I know the plans I have for you," declares the Lord,
"plans to prosper you and not to harm you,
plans to give you hope and a future."
Jeremiah 29:11

Today I sat in a meeting for over two hours. This particular gathering of our military headquarters staff was a "Senior Plans Meeting." This is a regular conference where the plans for the conduct of our missions (combat as well as humanitarian) are reviewed with the Commanding General, Lieutenant General Odierno. It allows him and other senior leaders to interject final changes and adjustments before the missions are carried out. Because what we do is literally a matter of life or death, it is important to have a solid plan. Soldiers do better when they trust and have confidence in the plans of their leaders.

How comforting it is to read from the book of Jeremiah and realize that God has a plan for us. It is a plan in which we can have complete confidence. When I left Fort Hood and headed for Iraq, my oldest daughter slipped a card into my bag. The card itself was humorous, but inside was a note from my daughter where she had written today's verse from Jeremiah 29:11. She also wrote this was *"her verse"* for our family that year. Just reading her words and then reading the verse deeply encouraged me.

I don't think the phrase *"to prosper you"* means that Christians should expect to automatically be rich or never have any problems. That kind of belief or philosophy is not Biblical; it does not match with Scripture. However, when taken in context, this Scripture tells us that we can count on God to love us and never forget us. It also communicates that we will prosper when we follow God's ways; ways that are unimaginably good. You can stand confident; trusting in God and knowing that God has a plan for your life. God's desire is to bless you.

The words of the reckless pierce like swords,
but the tongue of the wise brings healing.
Proverbs 12:18

Today's battlefield headquarters are much different than what you see in the old war movies. Computers and other high tech equipment are prominent throughout the headquarters. In our MNC-I Joint Operation Center (JOC), the dominant elements are tiered rows of computers, allowing multiple operators to see the three giant projection screens at the front of the JOC. Those screens are used to view reports, maps, charts, and other pertinent information during the briefings and to track the battlefield's operations as close to the time they are happening as possible. Through the use of high level technology and powerful computers we are able to view video feeds from satellites or aircraft and see enemy positions or activity as it happens.

When the JOC computers sit idle for a few minutes, a screen saver is activated. In our headquarters the screen saver function contains messages about the need for Operational Security (OPSEC). The messages are meant to keep us vigilant in maintaining the security/secrecy of what we do. One of the messages that pops-up is a picture of a Soldier and words that state, "If you talk too much, this man may die." Other messages show Soldiers that have been ambushed by the enemy and the phrases, "Someone must have talked," and "OPSEC – A careless word can cost a life."

The Bible also talks about the importance of being careful of what we say. The words we speak can bring comfort and encouragement, or if carelessly used, can cause harm and pain. Be a person who watches his or her tongue and brings blessing. Decide today to encourage someone with your words of kindness. Commit yourself to not hurting anyone with the words that come from your mouth, and strive to speak words that encourage and heal those you speak with.

Be on your guard; stand firm in the faith; be courageous; be strong.
Do everything in love.
1 Corinthians 16:13-14

One of our reports today was about a mounted patrol that stopped along a road to investigate what was thought to be an improvised explosive device (IED). As the Soldiers got out of their vehicles to conduct the investigation and establish security, a single shot from a sniper killed one of the Soldiers. This was not the first time this technique was used by the enemy. They emplaced something that looked like an IED, but it was really a trap to draw our Soldiers into danger.

This tactic is not a new one. In fact, satan has been using the same scheme for a long time, and Christians in the church have often fallen. The greatest example I can think of is when generally well-meaning believers identify what they think is an important issue. They begin to investigate or address the issue. It may be something truly significant like how (or if) to help the homeless. It might be about a Christian's approach to abortion. It might be something less significant; like the color of carpet in the church, more or less contemporary music in the worship service, or the order of worship.

The sniper round that often wounds or kills the church or members of the church is often not the issue which they are addressing. The real problem becomes the anger, and often hatred, that emerges as the issues are addressed. The enemy loves nothing more than seeing Christians fight one another or driving a wedge between believers. Don't be a part of the enemy's tactics. Stand for what you believe, but don't let it cause anger or bitterness in your life. Ask God to help you be a woman or man who is on guard for dangers and traps; one who stands firm in your faith, is courageous, strong, and acts with a spirit of love.

The brothers there had heard that we were coming, and
they traveled as far as the Forum of Appius
and the Three Taverns to meet us.
At the sight of these men Paul thanked God and was encouraged.
Acts 28:15

I'm getting ready to go visit some of the Religious Support Teams
(RSTs) that are outside of Baghdad, in the northern part of Iraq.
They fall under the command of the Multi-National Division-North
(MND-N), which reports to the command of the unit to which I'm
assigned, Multi-National Corp-Iraq (MNC-I). My trip is identified
as a "Staff Assistance Visit," which would indicate that the higher
headquarters (meaning me), is providing help/guidance/mentorship to
the subordinate level headquarters. Certainly, there is an element of this
as I've already been in communication with Ken Stice, the MND-N
Chaplain about issues we need to address and discuss.

Due to the position and rank I hold, there are some specific things
that I have to do regarding an issue or mission. There are also some
elements of operations where my role requires me to provide additional
direction. However, my primary intent is to encourage the MND-N
chaplains and chaplain assistants.

These men and women are at the very front lines, providing
religious support and pastoral care. They nurture the living, care for
the wounded (physically, emotionally, mentally, and spiritually), and
honor the dead. They are fully engaged; doing the best they can and
doing it well. It is hard, tiring, and draining work.

I realize that what they need most from me is encouragement. God
sees the same need in us. Obviously, providing guidance and direction
(with definite expectations) is part of God's plan. However, God's
primary desire is to encourage us with love, mercy, and grace. Allow
yourself to experience God's encouragement and then allow yourself
to be God's method of encouraging someone else.

"I am the good shepherd.
The good shepherd lays down his life for the sheep."
John 10:11

Flying low over the stark, barren, desert terrain, the flock of sheep was easily seen from the door of the Blackhawk helicopter in which I was riding. I had been in the air for almost an hour and this was not the first flock of sheep I'd seen. As a young boy, I spent a good amount of time on my Grandpa's farm. He raised both cattle and sheep, so I felt a little bit of connection with the shepherds who were leading the flocks moving across the landscape.

The shepherds of these flocks conjure an image of the shepherds found in the Bible. As we flew overhead, I could see the shepherd walking at the front of his flock. A few sheep were out in front but not too far away from him. A good number were right alongside the shepherd. Then the majority were following in a large group right behind him.

I imagine the shepherd knew his sheep and took great care to make sure they all remained within his sight. He knew which ones were the "up-front type" and which were the "I like to hang way back" type. Certainly, he had a way to account for all of his flock under his care; watching out for each one, protecting them, and ensuring that their basic needs were met.

Take heart, you who believe. Jesus is our great and loving shepherd, and we are His sheep whom He cares for and loves. His shepherding extends beyond anything else in the world. He is The Good Shepherd, and you can trust Him.

Take a few minutes to review the devotions you read during this past week. Write down three key lessons you learned. What aspect of the week's devotions resonates most with you? (If you are participating as a group or family take time to discuss these key lessons.)

_____

_____

_____

_____

Were there any aspects of the devotions that you had trouble identifying with? (If you are participating as a group or family take time to discuss the troubling portions.)

_____

_____

_____

_____

Write down names of people you know who might be struggling with some of the points from the devotions. Take time to pray for each person. (If you are participating as a group, or family take time to pray for the people identified.)

_____

_____

_____

_____

What changes do you feel God is calling you to make after reading last week's devotions? (If you are participating as a group or family take time to discuss those desired changes.)

_____

_____

_____

_____

Think about a personal example in your life that demonstrates the truth of the devotions. (If you are participating as a group or family take time to share some of the stories with each other.)

_____

_____

_____

_____

For the Lamb at the center of the throne will be their shepherd;
he will lead them to springs of living water. And God will
wipe away every tear from their eyes.
Revelation 7:17

Another of the very noticeable things that caught my attention while I was flying over the Iraqi landscape in the Blackhawk helicopter was the occurrence of green spots scattered amidst the brown, basically lifeless terrain. The green areas were so different and unique from the normal view, and they stood out from miles away as we flew along. It was amazing what took place in these dry, sandy areas, where the only change was the addition of water. The simple act of bringing water allowed the ground to produce beautiful areas in the midst of the desert, not to mention the flourishing of valuable agricultural crops.

Humanity is much like this. We are in need of spiritual water. We are by nature dried up, barren, and lifeless. We are often fooled into thinking we are just fine, or that we can care for (water) ourselves. It is only as we place ourselves in the hands of God (by accepting Jesus in our lives) that we begin to realize how dry and barren we really are.

What Jesus offers is living water, which allows us to truly grow and flourish. The transformation that God can bring to us is a true miracle. Like the transformation that water brings to a stark desert land, the coming of Jesus into the heart and life of a man or woman brings beautiful, eternal transformation.

Drink deeply from the living water that is found in Jesus. You will find yourself refreshed and flowing with renewed life.

Truly the righteous attain life, but whoever pursues evil finds death.
Proverbs 11:19

We knew it was coming. Saddam Hussein was being held here at Camp Victory, awaiting the outcome of his legal appeal. Most of us thought that the verdict would not come until after the first of the year, but it happened late in December. Then, wasting no time, the sentence of hanging was swiftly carried out. At 0617 (6:17 a.m.), Saddam Hussein was executed by the Iraqi government for crimes against his own people and humanity.

There were some people and groups who protested the execution. Later some small numbers of Iraqis mourned his death. However, the overwhelming majority seemed to agree that justice was served. Here in Iraq and around the world, pundits had wondered what would happen. Many had predicted upheaval, but those predictions of wide spread turmoil and violence did not come true.

I think most people, including both Sunni and Shia sects of Islam, knew what an evil man Saddam was. He was a dictator who ruled by terror and embraced injustice. Any person or group who opposed him, stood up to him, or simply displeased him was a good candidate for murder or torture.

Proverbs 11:19 tells us what Saddam's fate had to be. Even if he had lived a long life and died of old age, he would be lost to death eternally without Jesus in his life.

God calls us to righteousness, and we should strive for that goal. We are given life…eternal life…because of inviting Jesus into our life.

He refreshes my soul. He guides me along
the right paths for his name's sake.
Psalm 23:3

A few days ago, I wrote about flying over the country in a helicopter and seeing sheep with their shepherds. I'd like to spend a little more time on that concept using the 23rd Psalm, which tells us that God is our Shepherd. Because God is our Shepherd, certain things happen or come to us.

One of the things our Shepherd does is restore our souls. Let me explain. This simple concept could be looked at many ways, but I want to take the following view. Day after day we get casualty reports: U.S. Soldiers killed, Marines killed, Iraqi Army soldiers killed, even civilians killed. It can be extremely disheartening.

About three weeks ago, a wonderful female Marine who worked here in our Joint Operations Center and who loved to laugh and run long distance races (like me), was killed. Her death brought us close to 3,000 U.S. service members killed in theater. This kind of news can make one's heart weary.

In these type of instances, I look to God for comfort, peace, and some sense of renewal…and God does it. I'm not sure how, but as this great Psalm says, "God refreshes my soul." It is not something I take lightly or fully understand, but God accomplishes it.

Although I don't completely comprehend it, I know how much God's comfort, peace and renewal is needed here among our fine Soldiers who witness the day-to-day horror of war. I also know you need it in your life. Be restored! Trust God! Take a moment to thank God and ask "The Refresher of Souls" to renew your spirit.

Stand firm then, with the belt of truth buckled around your waist...
Ephesians 6:14a

Let's look again at how wearing God's armor can help us stand firm against the enemy. Evil is very real. In the spiritual realm, evil is embodied in the devil. The earthly realm has many forms of evil.

Terrorists who strike with no thought or care about others and are only concerned about themselves or their cause are an example of evil. Many of those terrorists make their acts even more heinous because they commit them in the guise of God's will or desire.

Another example of earthly evil is the multi-billion dollar pornography business in the United States and around the world that perpetuates human trafficking of innocent girls. What should be a wonderful, beautiful thing (the human body and the intimacy between a man and a woman) has been misused. Again, just as with terrorism, part of the tragedy is the people who profit from this use of half-truths and outright lies to justify their actions. Sadly, some of these folks begin to believe their own lies. They have exchanged a beautiful truth for an ugly lie.

This horrible business preys upon the weakness and tendency of humanity to sin. It is tempting to follow the desire for pleasure or supposed fulfillment, but both are fleeting, wrong, and cause harm. One of the lies of pornography says it doesn't hurt anyone...*but it does*.

These two examples of evil demonstrate our desperate need for God's first element of spiritual armor; the belt of truth around our waist. Truth, God's truth, needs to be the foundation of all we do and is the base element for true justice.

Stand firm then, with the belt of truth buckled around your waist,
with the breastplate of righteousness in place...
Ephesians 6:14

The personal body armor that all Soldiers now wear has resulted in fewer deaths of our Soldiers. The armor has been greatly improved over time and especially in the last five or six years. We now have plates made of special material that cover both the front and back of our upper-body torso. The plates are called ESAPI, which stands for Enhanced Small Arms Protective Insert.

These plates are vitally important because they provide significant protection for our internal organs; especially our hearts. They guard this key organ that pumps life blood throughout our bodies. Because of increased protection to vital organs, more Soldiers are surviving, but men and women are losing legs and arms. This is somewhat attributable to the ESAPI plates that now save a person's life. Previously Soldiers would have died because of the trauma to their body, but now they survive. Trauma is reduced in the critical areas around the chest but not in the exposed arms and legs; thus, we have more amputees.

Protecting the heart is essential for physical and spiritual survival. This is why part of God's armor includes a breastplate that guards and protects the heart. The call to live righteously, living in a way that is right in God's eyes, helps protect our hearts from fatal pain and injury.

My best tip for living righteously? Treat others as you want them to treat you; with kindness, dignity, compassion, respect, love, grace, and mercy.

Stand firm then, with the belt of truth buckled around your waist,
with the breastplate of righteousness in place,
and with your feet fitted with the readiness
that comes from the gospel of peace.
Ephesians 6:14-15

As I prepared for the convoy trip to a Forward Operating Base in Baghdad, I have to admit I was a little anxious. The violence in the city is amazing. It is common for the different sectarian groups to capture/kidnap each other, torture their victims, and then execute them by beheading.

Recently, we found kidnapped men who had holes drilled in them with an electric drill before they were beheaded and one person had been cut in half. Repeatedly witnessing the evidence of torture, plus the high incidence of improvised explosive devices emplaced along the roads, as well as unexpected sniper and rocket fire, would make most people anxious.

What does this have to do with the call to have, "feet fitted with the readiness that comes from the gospel of peace?" While I was going through the Army's Ranger School, one of the things that took some getting used to was sleeping in my boots. On those nights in the field when we would actually get some sleep, we followed specific protocol to ensure we'd be in a state of readiness. After drying our feet, we would put on dry socks and then put our boots back on. In the middle of the night it is almost impossible to react quickly and efficiently (readiness) if your boots are not on your feet.

Spiritually, God is telling us that the equivalent of boots is the peace of accepting and knowing Jesus Christ. If we are filled with anxiety or fear, if we are always on edge, then we are not really ready to fight against evil or to stand up for God. Walk with the assurance of the peace that Jesus can bring to your life.

...and do not give the devil an opportunity.
Ephesians 4:27

Engines roaring, the plane shoots off the runway and begins an almost vertical climb into the Iraqi sky. The manner in which our military planes take off and land is much different than the methods you see in the United States at one of our major commercial airports. Long, straight approaches to an airport with a gradual descent over miles of hostile territory are not tactically acceptable. The same holds true of planes departing the combat area. If there is too much exposure during these critical times, the enemy is much more likely to take shots at the aircraft.

During recent flights in our area of operations, I flew in a mode of air travel different from the helicopters that I normally utilized. I have often watched our fighter jets take-off; it is amazing seeing them literally jump off the runways, and then go into a straight vertical climb, with the flames shooting from the powerful jet engines. Even though I'd been briefed by the crew of the aircraft that the plane in which we were flying had similar take-off patterns as the jets, I was not fully prepared for our plane to climb and descend as rapidly and steeply as it did. In fact, our landings were "better" than an amusement park ride, especially since the "thrill" was not artificially produced. The reality of the flight and its risk was very tangible. The reason for the tactical landings and take-offs is because the threat is very real. The intent is to deny the enemy the opportunity to engage our aircraft.

We would do well to remember that our spiritual threat is very real. We must be careful not to grow complacent in our lives as we go about our daily activities. Don't put yourself in positions and places that allow you to be easily targeted by the enemy. Deny evil the opportunity to impact you by making wise and Godly decisions about who you associate with and where you spend your time.

Take a few minutes to review the devotions you read during this past week. Write down three key lessons you learned. What aspect of the week's devotions resonates most with you? (If you are participating as a group or family take time to discuss these key lessons.)

_____

_____

_____

_____

Were there any aspects of the devotions that you had trouble identifying with? (If you are participating as a group or family take time to discuss the troubling portions.)

_____

_____

_____

_____

Write down names of people you know who might be struggling with some of the points from the devotions. Take time to pray for each person. (If you are participating as a group, or family take time to pray for the people identified.)

_____

_____

_____

_____

What changes do you feel God is calling you to make after reading last week's devotions? (If you are participating as a group or family take time to discuss those desired changes.)

_____

_____

_____

_____

Think about a personal example in your life that demonstrates the truth of the devotions. (If you are participating as a group or family take time to share some of the stories with each other.)

_____

_____

_____

_____

Attacks and violence were a way of life for our Soldiers.
Rocket and mortar attacks were very common. The
photo above was taken by Chaplain Tarvin
following a rocket attack at the base where he served in Iraq.

Insurgents were constantly emplacing explosives. This attack was larger than
normal. The insurgents blew up the Sarafiya Bridge in Baghdad and
sent it crashing into the muddy waters of the Tigris River. Chaplain Tarvin was
traveling with General Odierno (Commanding General of the Multi-National
Corps-Iraq) and
took this picture from Odierno's helicopter.

Many people visited our Soldiers in both Iraq and Afghanistan.
This picture shows Chaplain Tarvin presenting a Bible to Bill O'Reilly.

Senator John McCain and Senator Lindsey Graham
were in Iraq. This is a picture of Senator McCain and Chaplain Tarvin.

Secretary of Defense Donald Rumsfeld attended a Christmas service and is
pictured with Chaplain Tarvin who preached the service.

Memorial Ceremonies and Memorial Walls were far too common in both Iraq and Afghanistan. Above is a Memorial Ceremony set-up for five great Soldiers and friends at Camp Victory.

These types of Memorial Walls were found at many of our camps and Forward Operating Bases (FOBs). This Wall of Heroes is located at FOB Warhorse and is in memory of the Soldiers who were Killed in Action from the units that served there.

(left to right) – Chaplain (Colonel) Tarvin, SSG Solorio, Chaplain (Major) Arauco

Third Day, the Grammy and Dove award winning Christian Rock Band, played to troops all over Iraq. Here Chaplain Tarvin poses with the Band.

In addition to all this, take up the shield of faith,
with which you can extinguish all the flaming arrows of the evil one.
Ephesians 6:16

There are numerous threats to our Soldiers in Iraq. Two of the greatest threats are improvised explosive devices (IEDs) and sniper fire. IEDs take many different forms. Among the most common are the bombs that are placed alongside the road and are detonated as our vehicles drive by or over the bomb. There are also vehicle borne IEDs (VBIEDs); where explosives are placed in a vehicle and the vehicle is detonated when people get near it. Another deadly threat is a suicide VBIED (SVBIED); where the vehicle is driven by a suicide driver into a group of people or a target. There are other variations with the IEDs, but you get the idea. A sniper is an individual with a rifle and a scope who targets our Soldiers from long distances and strikes them in the few areas where they don't have body armor.

To help guard against these two types of enemy attacks, we have made special additions to our vehicles that I view at as our modern-day *shields*. The additional armor and reinforced glass, along with the armored cupola on the top of the vehicle, have saved the lives of many of our Soldiers. The sniper's bullets and the shrapnel from the IEDs are now often rendered useless; unable to penetrate the shield of armor or glass.

Faith, a strong determined belief, is our spiritual shield. The evil one's attempts to assault us can't penetrate a strong shield of faith in our Lord. Develop your faith. Hold firm to it and many of life's assaults will be repelled.

Take the helmet of salvation...
Ephesians 6:17a

All of our military equipment has undergone changes and improvements over the years. Some of the most dramatic and visual changes have been in the evolution of the helmet. One of the ways to identify the era of a Soldier is to look at the helmet on their head.

The broad-rimmed helmet is a giveaway for World War One Soldiers, and the steel pot of World War Two is also easily identified. By the time the Army parachuted into Panama and hit the sands in Desert Storm, the helmet not only had a new look that offered more coverage, but used materials that made it stronger and better. Today our helmets are even more impenetrable, lighter, and have their own unique design.

Everyone knows a bullet, shrapnel, or even just a strong blow to an unprotected head can easily be fatal. It is the reason I always wear a helmet when I ride my Harley (motorcycle). It is also why Soldiers want good helmets and are quick to put them on. Wearing a helmet brings a much higher assurance of life. I don't think I've ever heard a Soldier going outside the "wire" (the protected area of encampment) say, "I don't think I'll wear my helmet today." They want to live, so they put on their helmets.

That is why salvation is identified as our Spiritual helmet. It brings a complete assurance of life...eternal life. Our willingness to trust Jesus and surrender our life to God by accepting Jesus as our Lord is equivalent to putting on the "helmet of salvation."

If you are reading this and have never asked Jesus into your heart I want to encourage you to do so now. Simply say, "God, I want to be in relationship with you, I accept Jesus as my Lord and Savior and place my trust in Him." You have "put on the helmet of salvation," now find a church or a mature Christian who can help you better understand and live out this wonderful decision.

Take the helmet of salvation and
the sword of the Spirit, which is the word of God.
Ephesians 6:17

As an Army Chaplain there is one major difference between me
and other Soldiers. The Chaplain is the only Soldier who does not carry
a weapon. We are non-combatants. Some people think it is dangerous
not to carry a weapon when we are with our fellow Soldiers in the
midst of the fight. However, a weapon is not needed for the chaplains
to fulfill their role.

In combat, as well as peace-time, the primary focus of the chaplain
is to nurture the living, care for the wounded, and honor the dead by
providing pastoral care to Soldiers. When men and women are fighting
and dying the chaplains have plenty to do. Ministering to the Soldiers,
Sailors, Airmen, and Marines is a full-time endeavor. Caring for them
is our mission, and chaplains don't need to be kinetically involved in
the fighting.

Our ability to conduct our ministry is partially based on the fire
power around us. Every chaplain has a chaplain assistant who carries
a weapon. In addition to their many responsibilities part of every
chaplain assistant's duty is to provide protection for the chaplain.

I recently traveled with a convoy that had four gun vehicles, In
addition, each vehicle in the convoy was heavily armed. It is that fire
power that really enables us to get out and be among the people, in the
midst of the enemy. It gives Soldiers a sense of confidence to make a
stand and not feel as if they will be unable to defend themselves and
those they are supposed to protect.

The final part of our spiritual armor is our weapon; the sword of
the Spirit. It empowers us as Christians. What made the early disciples
change from fear and trembling to emboldened proclaimers of Christ?
It was the Holy Spirit. The Spirit lives in us and is our weapon to fight
evil.

I have been crucified with Christ and I no longer live,
but Christ lives in me.
The life I now live in the body, I live by faith in the Son of God,
who loved me and gave himself for me.
Galatians 2:20

Soldiers who have participated in combat operations are awarded the honor of wearing the insignia of the unit with whom they served in combat on the right shoulder of their uniform. These insignia (patches) are worn on a Soldier's left shoulder while that Soldier is assigned to the unit. The insignia are worn permanently on the right shoulder of a Soldier's uniform no matter where they are assigned in the future.

The patches themselves are all unique, and each one incorporates something about the unit. Other Soldiers can look at someone's patch and tell what type of unit he or she is currently assigned. For instance, airborne units have an airborne tab located at the top of their patch, so that anyone who looks at them will know they are part of an airborne unit.

The other night we conducted a small ceremony at Multi-National Corps-Iraq headquarters. All Soldiers from our unit put the MNC-I patch on their right shoulder. During the ceremony the Commanding General, LTG Odierno, addressed the unit. He talked about the significance of the ceremony and how it marked our specific and special affiliation with Multi-National Corps-Iraq and the U.S. Army III Corps. He pointed out the commitment combat demanded and the bond that it created.

I began to think that Christianity should have the same result. Deciding to accept Jesus and serve God is the most significant act anyone can do. It calls for us to make a big commitment and should result in a deep bond with other believers. Those aspects serve as part of our Christian "patch," a sign of our affiliation with Jesus.

Then these men went as a group and found Daniel praying and
asking God for help.
Daniel 6:11 -

I was part of a mission through a dangerous part of Baghdad that
caused me to think about another important aspect of our spiritual life.
We need to incorporate spiritual facets of life that help keep us safe.

As we drove through the city, some key equipment in our vehicles
stopped working. As hard as it was to believe, the Plugger (a global
positioning device-GPS) in each vehicle went down one by one. This
device tells the user his location, and if the drivers and those in charge
have not tracked movement well on the map, a Plugger can help find
the way because it is easy to get lost.

That is exactly what happened; we got lost in Baghdad. I was
listening in on the internal communication system and was able to
hear the NCOs say, "My GPS is down." Then another vehicle reported
the same thing. There was a call asking if anyone's GPS was working.
The answer was no, and then the lead vehicle asked if anyone knew
where we were.

The senior Sergeant in my vehicle said he thought we had missed
our turn about two blocks back. So we made a U-turn. We ended up
making three U-turns in the next 20-30 minutes. We eventually had
to stop in a very dangerous area of Baghdad to do a good map recon
(reconnaissance/check). We eventually figured out where we were and
then made it to our destination. I was impressed that the leader in the
front asked for help, admitting he was lost.

God calls us to do the same thing. When you are in trouble, when
you are lost, call on God for help. Trying to do it all on your own only
leads to increased problems. Call on God for Help!

As a fair exchange—I speak as to my children—
open wide your hearts also.
2 Corinthians 6:13 -

Not too long ago, I wrote about God's Armor and the protection it offers, compared to the body armor Soldiers wear. There are other methods we use to provide protection for our Soldiers.

One of those methods is the emplacement of large concrete barriers around buildings and areas that don't have a good structural protection. My original office was in a building that was part of the overall palace complex and was constructed of large stones and masonry. It was a beautiful, sturdy, secure, and protective building. At one point we turned that building back over to the Iraqi Army. I, along with my staff, moved to a new structure made of plywood and drywall, not quite as protective as stone and masonry. Anyone remember the three little pigs?

So, in order to help prevent rocket or mortar fire possibly impacting on or near this less durable building, large concrete barriers were placed around it. This effort not only protects us physically, but it also makes us feel emotionally more secure. We believe that we are safer behind these large walls, and thus our emotional security increases.

Sometimes walls protect, but at times they also isolate and prevent needed communication. We often do that with our personal lives. We erect emotional barriers around our hearts and refuse to let others or God get too close. Often we erect these internal barriers because we have been hurt in the past, but the solution of giant walls around our hearts is too drastic. Paul encouraged his readers to open their hearts. Lower some of your walls, open your heart, and let God and others who can love you into your life.

Live a life of love, just as Christ loved us and
gave himself up for us as a fragrant offering and sacrifice to God.
Ephesians 5:2

Three days ago one of our helicopters was shot down by a portable ground-to-air rocket/missile system. Twelve men and women on board were killed, and four of those twelve were from our headquarters here in Baghdad. The senior-ranking member was a friend whom I usually saw every day. Four other Soldiers on that helicopter were friends of mine. It was a great loss.

The Chaplains in the theater of war do great ministry across a wide spectrum. Our Army chaplain mandate (mission statement) is the following: *Nurture the living; Care for the wounded; and Honor the dead.* The chaplains provide worship services, sacraments, pastoral counseling, ministry/humanitarian opportunities, and many other programs and ministries. Most of what we do is enjoyable and rewarding, but one aspect is definitely not enjoyable. When one of our fellow Soldiers dies, we honor the Soldier by conducting a memorial ceremony.

As we prepare for these memorial ceremonies, we try to learn as much as we can about the Soldiers who have been killed. Talking to friends and co-workers who knew the Soldiers provides the greatest insight. As people talked about this wonderful senior officer we lost in the helicopter that was shot down, it became clear that he was a man of faith and honor who loved God, family, others, and country.

What will people say about you when you die? Will you be remembered and honored as a person of faith and integrity. Will you be recognized as woman or man who loved God and others? Make this a goal, not just for the sake of having people say good things, but because of your commitment to be a person of genuine faith who loves God and others.

Take a few minutes to review the devotions you read during this past week. Write down three key lessons you learned. What aspect of the week's devotions resonates most with you? (If you are participating as a group or family take time to discuss these key lessons.)

_____

_____

_____

_____

Were there any aspects of the devotions that you had trouble identifying with? (If you are participating as a group or family take time to discuss the troubling portions.)

_____

_____

_____

_____

Write down names of people you know who might be struggling with some of the points from the devotions. Take time to pray for each person. (If you are participating as a group, or family take time to pray for the people identified.)

_____

_____

_____

_____

What changes do you feel God is calling you to make after reading last week's devotions? (If you are participating as a group or family take time to discuss those desired changes.)

_____

_____

_____

_____

Think about a personal example in your life that demonstrates the truth of the devotions. (If you are participating as a group or family take time to share some of the stories with each other.)

_____

_____

_____

_____

On reaching the place, he said to them,
"Pray that you will not fall into temptation."
Luke 22:40

The importance and power of prayer has often been reinforced during my extended time in Iraq and limited time in Afghanistan. I have experienced it in my own life and Soldiers have shared numerous stories about answered prayer in their lives. It is encouraging to hear accounts from men and women who have seen prayer have a positive impact on their life.

Recently, I wrote about a ground convoy trip to a Forward Operating Base (FOB). Today, in the Battle Update Brief, there was a report about this same FOB. The briefer reported a recent attack on the FOB that caused two deaths and six wounded. That FOB can be a dangerous place, and the route to get there is often hazardous as well. Add to that our convoy getting off track and ending up in some even more treacherous parts of Baghdad, and you have a recipe for disaster. We were in a very bad situation. Yet, despite some close calls, our trip concluded with no casualties.

Shortly after I made this trip, I wrote a letter describing our experience to some family and friends. A number of them wrote back, reinforcing their commitment of praying for me and our Soldiers. However, the best reply was during a phone call with my wife just a couple days after the incident. She said that during the time I was on the convoy, she was at home and had felt the need to do something unusual.

She prays for me regularly, but this day she felt compelled by God to get out of bed just after mid-night and fervently pray for several hours for my safety and wellbeing. This was the exact same time that my convoy was engaged in a very bad situation in Sadr City. Sadr City was the center of power for the insurgent Mahdi Army in Baghdad. We were in desperate need of prayer, and God stirred her heart at just the right moment.

What a wonderful strength and support prayer can be. Be a prayer warrior for your family and friends. It does make a difference.

Here is my servant whom I have chosen, the one I love, in whom I delight;
I will put my Spirit on him, and he will proclaim justice to the nations.
Matthew 12:18

Not too long ago I spent a day in the International Zone (IZ) of Baghdad. While I was there I met with a number of people and sat through some briefings. However, the most impactful time was spent at the combat support hospital (CSH).

This essential facility is sometimes referred to as "Baghdad ER." Be assured it is much more than just an ER...although the emergency room there handles the worst of the worst and does a magnificent job. The staff who work at the hospital are amazing men and women. They are dedicated to caring for our Soldiers who have been wounded or injured. They are true servants; giving themselves completely to the Soldiers they care for.

While we were at the IZ, we came under attack by rocket fire and a vehicle borne improvised explosive device. This seems to be a common occurrence in the IZ. Yet, the efforts of the medical personnel are not reduced in the least. If anything, the men and women who work at the CSH respond to these dangers and medical traumas with an even greater commitment to serve.

I was able to pray with one of our Soldiers being treated for wounds he received from an IED that destroyed his vehicle and killed the driver. During the prayer the medics paused and then said their "amens" when I finished the prayer.

Real servants recognize the true Master (God) and know that their ultimate service is to God. Jesus understood the need and role of being a servant before God. We are called to incorporate the same type of servant attitude in our lives and care for those God places in our life.

Just as each of us has one body with many members, and these members
do not all have the same function,
so in Christ we who are many form one body,
and each member belongs to all the others.
Romans 12:4-5

A few days ago, I wrote about a memorial ceremony we were preparing to conduct. That ceremony was held at our headquarters the other night. We had every chair available, about two hundred, set up for those wishing to attend the ceremony.

The ceremony was scheduled to begin at 2030 (8:30 p.m.). Those of us who were actually participating gathered at 2000 hours (8:00 p.m.). As I walked out to the area where the ceremony would take place, I was a little surprised to see that at least one half of the seats were already filled, and people were arriving in a steady stream.

We were honoring and remembering five of our fallen warriors from our little work area of Camp Victory. Four of the Soldiers were from my headquarters of Multi-National Corps-Iraq and one was from Multi-National Forces-Iraq. For most of us, it was like losing family members, and so people came and came and came. Between four and five hundred people ended up attending, quite a testimonial to the five Soldiers from our community who had died.

The bond that exists between Soldiers, especially those serving in the common cause of justice and freedom through combat, results in such great unity and support. It is something that most people outside of the Army won't totally experience, but there are similar bonding experiences in life.

One place where we should see a similar bond is the one between brothers and sisters in Christ. We are called to be one body, working together for the common cause of Christ and ultimate freedom. Are you part of a community of faith? If you are not, you are missing out on an essential aspect of God's plan for your support and well-being. Find a gathering of Christians where you can be taught, nurtured, and enjoy fellowship with other believers.

Abraham was now old and well advanced in years,
and the Lord had blessed him in every way. He said to the senior
servant in his household, the one in charge of all that he had,
"Put your hand under my thigh.
I want you to swear by the Lord, the God of heaven and the God of
earth, that you will not get a wife for my son from the daughters of
the Canaanites, among whom I am living, but will go to my country
and my own relatives and get a wife for my son Isaac."
Genesis 24: 1-4

Not long ago I wrote about the servant oriented medical staff at the combat support hospital who give so much of themselves to provide care for our Soldiers. It got me thinking about what makes a good servant.

The story in Genesis about the servant who was given the mission of finding a wife for Abraham's son Isaac, provides keen insight about this key concept of Christian living. As you read the scriptural narrative it becomes apparent he possessed the attributes of a good servant. The story centers on Isaac and Rebekah, but for a brief period, we follow this servant. What he does and says provides some good insight about what makes a worthy servant of God.

First, we notice that this servant has a relationship with the master, Abraham. He has proven himself and is referred to as a being trusted. The servant is given this very important mission, and he is provided all the resources he needs to accomplish what the Master has called him to do.

This story calls us to be the type of servant Abraham sends out to find a bride for his son, Isaac. The servant represents us as humanity. Abraham, the master, is representative of God. Going out and finding "brides" for his Son is part of God's desire for us as His servants. God calls us as servants and gives us all we need to be the type of men and women God desires us to be. There are additional key aspects that are part of our mission as God's servants that I will cover in the next few days.

The servant asked him, "What if the woman is unwilling to come back with me to this land? Shall I then take your son back to the country you came from?" "Make sure that you do not take my son back there," Abraham said. "The Lord, the God of heaven, who brought me out of my father's household and my native land and who spoke to me and promised me on oath, saying…'he will send his angel before you so that you can get a wife for my son from there. If the woman is unwilling to come back with you, then you will be released from this oath of mine.

Genesis 24: 5-8

The military in Iraq has numerous roles. Combat operations are a part of what we do, and we do it well. However, we also spend a lot of time and effort in humanitarian, economic, and diplomatic endeavors.

One of the goals of our humanitarian-type operations, is to demonstrate our good intentions to the overall populace. We have established several centers, throughout Iraq and Afghanistan, which provide clothing, food, and other needed supplies. The mission of those who run the centers is to make sure the centers are secure, have the resources they need, and are ready to provide services. They are not called to coerce or compel the locals to come and take advantage of this opportunity.

The servant in our story of Isaac and Rebekah almost got off track in his mission concerning the same thing. He had his mission, but he was worried about finding the right person. He was also concerned that if he found the right woman she might not want to come with him. The Master assured him he only had to do what he had been called to do. He only needed to focus on his mission, and the responsibility he was given.

God calls us to much the same thing. Sometimes we worry too much about the reactions of those we are called to care for or minister to. Our focus should be on the actual mission and leave the results up to God. Don't allow your eyes to focus on peripheral issues; remain fixed on the primary goal God has given you, whatever that might be.

Then the servant left, taking with him ten of his master's camels loaded with all kinds of good things from his master. He set out for Aram Naharaim and made his way to the town of Nahor. He had the camels kneel down near the well outside the town; it was toward evening, the time the women go out to draw water.

Genesis 24: 10-11

Whenever we have a convoy going out on a mission, the leaders of the group will check in by radio with our operations staff. One of the critical checks they will accomplish is determining the status of the route they are taking. This same type of check is done each time the convoy gets on a new portion of a route. The route may be classified as green, which indicates no problems. However, there are times when the route is amber (moderate risk) or even red (extreme risk). These classifications are based on criteria such as recent attacks or threats in the area. Depending on how bad a route is, the convoy may be directed to a less risky road to help ensure the safety and success of the mission.

The servant who went to get a bride for Isaac also wanted to put himself in the best position for success. He set some conditions so that he would know if he was on track. He then placed himself in a location where those conditions could best be met. He went to the community well, where he knew that the local young women would come at the end of the day in order to get water. Not only would he find women at the well, but they would be women who were able and willing to work.

Are you putting yourself in position for success, or are you doing the opposite? Are the places you spend time conducive to success? Are you hanging out in places where you are likely to do something you will regret? Are the people with whom you spend time or the places you frequent a help or hindrance to your call and purpose in life? Resolve to put yourself in a position to succeed, and to associate with people who will most likely be men and women of good character.

After she had given him a drink, she said,
"I'll draw water for your camels too,
until they have had enough to drink." So she quickly emptied her jar
into the trough, ran back to the well to draw more water,
and drew enough for all his camels.
Genesis 24: 19-20

The Army has standards for just about everything. One of the areas in which every Soldier is called to meet the standard is physical fitness. The numbers of push-ups and sit-ups a Soldier does and how fast a Soldier runs two miles determines the number of points scored. The minimum score a Soldier can attain and pass is 180 points, and no single event can be less than 60 out of 100 points. Three hundred points is the maximum score for the fitness test.

I always try to score 300 points. I don't always make it, but most of the time I do. It requires me to do about seventy push-ups and seventy sit-ups and run two miles in under fourteen minutes. Some Soldiers only strive for the minimum, just enough to pass. A majority try to do their very best, going beyond the minimum and striving for the maximum score.

Both the servant and Rebekah went beyond the minimum. They were determined to give their best effort, the maximum. Rebekah, not only offered to bring water for the camels of the servant, but she agreed to bring water until the camels were satisfied; that is a lot of water.

God calls us to do our best in whatever it is we do, not to be content with just getting by, but striving for the maximum. Don't settle for okay; decide to be the best husband, the best mother, the best daughter, the best son, the best leader, the best employee, the best student, the best church member, or the best "whatever" you can. My parents raised me with an old axiom that I have slightly altered. "If something is worth doing, it is worth doing to the best of your ability."

Take a few minutes to review the devotions you read during this past week. Write down three key lessons you learned. What aspect of the week's devotions resonates most with you? (If you are participating as a group or family take time to discuss these key lessons.)

_____

_____

_____

_____

Were there any aspects of the devotions that you had trouble identifying with? (If you are participating as a group or family take time to discuss the troubling portions.)

_____

_____

_____

_____

Write down names of people you know who might be struggling with some of the points from the devotions. Take time to pray for each person. (If you are participating as a group, or family take time to pray for the people identified.)

_____

_____

_____

_____

What changes do you feel God is calling you to make after reading last week's devotions? (If you are participating as a group or family take time to discuss those desired changes.)

_____

_____

_____

_____

Think about a personal example in your life that demonstrates the truth of the devotions. (If you are participating as a group or family take time to share some of the stories with each other.)

_____

_____

_____

_____

But God has put the body together giving greater honor to the
parts that lacked it, so that there should be no division in the body,
but that its parts should have equal concern for each other.
1 Corinthians 12: 24b-25

At the Corps staff level we receive many actions to which we
have to respond, and we are expected to produce numerous products.
To do it all as an individual or even with just a few people would be
impossible. I rely on a great team of Chaplains and Chaplain Assistants
in my office to run the Multi-National Corps-Iraq Chaplain operation.
We are very conscious about coordinating actions with other staff
departments. We also make sure we are aware of what each person is
doing that might impact the others.

I remember a family trip we once took to visit relatives in California.
We were living in Tacoma, Washington, and drove to the San Francisco
area. We camped along the way and had the great thrill of hiking
through parts of the National Redwood Forest. The tall magnificent
trees are amazing to see. I discovered that their ability to grow so tall
and not topple over in bad storms is due in large part to their root
systems that inter-connect with other trees around the forest. This
connection creates a team type of mutual support. Where one or two
trees might not be able to stand; the group depends on and helps one
another. Not only do they stand and survive, they thrive, growing into
beautiful and amazing trees that live for hundreds of years.

It is important for us to be connected with a church, a study group,
family, friends, co-workers, and others. A supportive and caring team
is important in life. Being part of a supportive group or team that
cares about each other often helps us to weather life's storms. Are you
standing alone or with little sustenance? God is calling you to be a part
of the most supportive and caring team there is: God's team.

Therefore, as God's chosen people, holy and dearly loved, clothe
yourselves with compassion, kindness, humility, gentleness and patience.
Colossians 3:12

Valentine's Day can be a wonderful time to celebrate the relationship
between those who have a strong love for one another. It can also
serve to simply convey a sense caring for another person. Here in Iraq
we received many Valentine cards from people in the U.S. to let the
Soldiers, Sailors, Airmen, and Marines know someone is thinking
about them, cares about them, and is praying for them.

However, Valentine's Day can be a sad day for those who don't
receive any cards or gifts. They may feel as if no one cares. For our
Soldiers in combat, who are separated for a long period of time and
can't spend Valentine's Day with those they love, it can be an especially
difficult day. It is hard to go through a year and miss all the major
events in your loved ones and families' lives. Birthdays, anniversaries,
Christmas, Hanukah, Easter, Fourth of July, Thanksgiving, and
graduations are all times and events military men and women deployed
to combat miss sharing with those they love. I am grateful that I have
a wonderful wife and family who love me. Not everyone is so blessed
to have others who love them. A lack of feeling loved and cared for can
make hard times even harder.

As Christians we have the comfort of a God who loves us. What
a joy and great assurance to know that God loves us. We can always
count on God's love, no matter where we are or in what circumstances
we find ourselves. Today and every day know you are loved, *dearly
loved*, by God. God's love for you knows no bounds. Nothing can
thwart God's love; no person, force, or organization can prevent you
from knowing and experiencing the love of God. If you don't know that
love, start today by asking Jesus to be the Savior of your life.

Day after day men came to help David, until he had a great army,
like the army of God. Men of Zebulun,
experienced soldiers prepared for battle
with every type of weapon, to help David with undivided loyalty.
1 Chronicles 12:22 & 33

Yesterday I wrote about God's deep, abiding, and ever-present love, no matter where we are physically located or our life circumstances. Today, I spoke at a prayer breakfast held at Camp Slayer in Baghdad. I taught on the principle of God's love, as well as the need for loyalty and service to others. The concept of loyalty is a key concept for many of our men and women in uniform. For Soldiers, loyalty is a gigantic issue. Soldiers need to feel that those above them are loyal to them and won't "hang them out" with no support. They also want their fellow Soldiers to know that they will be loyal to them, especially in the crucible of combat operations.

At the prayer breakfast, I used the story of Daniel and the lion's den to drive home a couple points of leadership. Loyalty was one of those points and was demonstrated by both Daniel and God. Daniel was trapped in a bad situation by some other leaders who were jealous of him. They lied to the king and got him to sign a decree that they knew Daniel would violate because of the loyalty he had consistently demonstrated in his relationship with God. They had manipulated a decree by the king that eliminated Daniel's ability to pray to God in order to trap Daniel and cause him to lose favor with the king and to be put to death.

Daniel knew that he would be in great danger, but he prayed anyway. He was loyal to God. As a result he paid a high cost and was thrown in the lion's den. Miraculously, God kept the lions from harming Daniel. Loyalty is an attribute demonstrated by God and one that God wants from us in our relationship with Him. As long as we are not violating an ethical or moral principle we should also be loyal to the men and women with whom we live and work.

Now when Daniel learned that the decree had been published, he went home to his upstairs room where the windows opened toward Jerusalem. Three times a day he got down on his knees and prayed, giving thanks to his God, just as he had done before.

Daniel 6: 10

I know I've written on the power and desire for prayer before, but I don't think I can adequately convey how valued prayer is for the men and women in this combat environment who go into harm's way every day. Prayer is as important to our spiritual life as water is to our physical being.

Yesterday, I wrote about my talk at a recent prayer breakfast and the lessons of loyalty from the story of Daniel and the lion's den. One of the other lessons from the same story focuses on prayer. Just like our Soldiers who value the prayers offered for them, Daniel placed a great value on prayer. His fellow leaders knew he was a man of prayer, and they plotted to use his commitment of regular prayer to trap him.

Yesterday's devotion focused on Daniel's loyalty to God and his willingness to continue to pray. However, in addition to the sense of loyalty, there was also the impact of the prayer that additionally pushed Daniel to pray, despite the King's decree. Daniel understood that without prayer and the continuing of his relationship with God by communicating in this manner, he was truly doomed. Daniel had a deep comprehension that prayer is how we maintain our communication and relationship with God. He understood that the inability to communicate with God through prayer would be worse than ending up in the lion's den.

Do you have this type of vision about your prayers? Regular prayer time, where we listen and talk to God, is the essential element for maintaining our relationship with God. Be a woman or man of prayer.

The heavens declare the glory of God;
the skies proclaim the work of his hands.
Day after day they pour forth speech;
night after night they reveal knowledge.
Psalm 19: 1-2

Baghdad, Iraq is an amazing place, especially on the outskirts of the city where our camp is located. Many days we can look across the landscape and see smoke rising from some point in the city. Most often it is smoke coming from the aftermath of an attack. However, there are also many days and numerous hours of every day when the horizon is clear. Most of those days are beautiful.

For most of the year there is not a lot of rain and also not many clouds. There is a lack of heavy industry as well, so the sky is normally a brilliant blue. At night, with limited lighting in our area, the clear skies reveal a dazzling array of stars. When I return to my little living area late at night, I like to look up at the heavens before I step inside my hootch and just enjoy the beauty of what God has provided. I often pause and think that my wife may be looking at the very same glorious stars.

Psalm 19 describes the same thing, *"The heavens declare the glory of God; the skies proclaim the work of His hands."* The Psalm ends with, *"May the words of my mouth and the meditation of my heart be pleasing in your sight, O Lord, my Rock and my Redeemer."*

Today, stop for just a moment and marvel at the beauty and wonder of God's creation. Enjoy the blue sky or a starlit night. Find a tall tree and take in the majesty of those branches stretching to the clouds above. Listen to the wind blow in the midst of a storm. The majesty and wonder of what God has created and entrusted to us is evident everywhere we turn. Enjoy it.

I waited patiently for the LORD; he turned to me and heard my cry.
He lifted me out of the slimy pit, out of the mud and mire;
he set my feet on a rock and gave me a firm place to stand.
Psalm 40:1-2 -

The rain has turned much of our camp into a large muddy mess. I recently flew with one of our generals to a Forward Operating Base (FOB) named Falcon. FOB Falcon was like a giant mud pit where the military vehicle traffic had worked the mud up to a thick, gooey quagmire. The mud pit reminded me of my time at the Army's elite Ranger School in 1977. There is an obstacle course at the school called the *Worm Pit*. At one point on the course, there are horizontal ladders (monkey bars) across a chest-deep pit that is filled with stagnant, scum filled water. The pit is dug in the red Georgian clay and dirt, and there is over a foot of pure muck at the bottom. One of the ladders spanning this nasty pit has a bar missing and always causes the Ranger crossing on that ladder to fall in the pit. One of the training sergeants always made me do that faulty ladder and thus fall in the gross water. If a Soldier fell in the pit he had to do push-ups under the water in the slime below.

Every day I would be directed to the same ladder and every day I ended up in the mud and mire. One day as I came up out of the water, I felt totally beaten. Blinking the slimy water out of my eyes, I looked up and my Ranger Buddy was reaching his hand down from the other side of the pit. He pulled me up, set me on the solid ground and said, "Come on, you can do this; don't let them get to you."

Psalm 40 says, *"I waited patiently for the Lord, He turned to me and heard my cry. He pulled me from the pit, from the mud and mire; he set my feet on a rock and gave me a firm place to stand."* We all end up in a "pit of mud and mire" from time to time and struggle to get out, sometimes needing help. God offers that help. Just as in the Psalm, Jesus has reached down with his nail-scarred hand to pull us to solid ground. Today, take the hand of Jesus and accept his help as the Savior and Lord of your life.

So we say with confidence, "The Lord is my helper; I will not be afraid.
What can mere mortals do to me?"
Hebrews 13:6

There are many Bible studies and fellowship groups that meet all over Afghanistan and Iraq. Soldiers, Sailors, Airmen and Marines meet in the different forward operating bases, combat outposts, and camps to study God's word and fellowship with one another. Yesterday, I attended one of those groups that meet in one of the dining facilities on Camp Liberty. The man who was teaching the lesson touched on a subject that impacts not only Soldiers but every person in the world. He talked about fear and the many detrimental effects that fear can bring. Fear can cause us to freeze or become immobile, not taking action when action is vital. It can also produce the opposite effect and cause us to do something we should not do.

A friend of mine was training some new lieutenants in Iraq and experienced the former reaction. He and the two lieutenants were unexpectedly faced with rifle fire from enemy insurgents. My friend immediately returned fire and killed two of three insurgents who were trying to kill him. In the process my friend was shot and wounded by the enemy fighters. Both of his legs had gunshot wounds, and he fell to the ground, bleeding and with a weapon that was now jammed. The two lieutenants were just behind him, but they froze and for a brief moment were not able to take action. At that same moment, the Sergeant Major arrived. He immediately went into action and successfully engaged the last enemy soldier, killing him just as he was taking aim at my helpless friend.

Don't let fear hold you back from actions you know you should take. Trust God to help you and give you the needed courage and strength.

Take a few minutes to review the devotions you read during this past week. Write down three key lessons you learned. What aspect of the week's devotions resonates most with you? (If you are participating as a group or family take time to discuss these key lessons.)

_____

_____

_____

_____

Were there any aspects of the devotions that you had trouble identifying with? (If you are participating as a group or family take time to discuss the troubling portions.)

_____

_____

_____

_____

Write down names of people you know who might be struggling with some of the points from the devotions. Take time to pray for each person. (If you are participating as a group, or family take time to pray for the people identified.)

_____

_____

_____

_____

What changes do you feel God is calling you to make after reading last week's devotions? (If you are participating as a group or family take time to discuss those desired changes.)

_____

_____

_____

_____

Think about a personal example in your life that demonstrates the truth of the devotions. (If you are participating as a group or family take time to share some of the stories with each other.)

_____

_____

_____

_____

Rejoice in the Lord always. I will say it again: Rejoice!
Philippians 4:4

Who in this world should be joyful? Perhaps those men and women with lots of money should be full of joy. The ability or opportunity to purchase whatever they desire ought to be a path to joy. Maybe it is those folks who are intelligent, or who have lots of friends. Surely those people should be joyful. Yet, we know that there are many rich, smart, and congenial people who are not joyful. Those things don't necessarily equate to joy. Although, once I did hear someone say that money may not buy happiness, but it sure does help. Sadly, too many people become disappointed when they realize joy is not found in money or power.

I met an Iraqi woman who was full of joy. Yet, she lived in desperate circumstances, in a country torn by civil strife; where murder, crime, and torture are a day-to-day reality. Still, she was excited about her life and truly joyful. She was getting ready to move back into war-torn Baghdad. When we talked, she shared she had chosen to be joyful in her circumstances and to rest in Jesus. Just being a Christian in Iraq can bring real danger, and would cause some people to lose or hide their joy.

Despite the tragedy around her, often impacting her personally, and the very real danger she faced because of her faith, this woman chose the path of joy. She chose joy because of the very faith that placed her in danger. She felt that God called her to live joyfully. Mother Teresa, the great missionary to India, once said, *"Let us always meet each other with a smile, for the smile is the beginning of love."*

What path are you choosing? It is a choice. Will you choose to reflect the joy of God who loved us so much he gave his Son Jesus? Meet others with a smile. Be joyful! Rejoice!

Who will listen to what you say? The share of the man who stayed with the supplies is to be the same as that of him who went down to the battle. All will share alike.

1 Samuel 30:24

There is a Soldier who comes by our offices now and again to pick up some reading material or just to talk. I knew him at Fort Hood before we came to Iraq. We ran together during the tryouts for the Foot Hood Army ten-mile race team. His primary job is serving as the Commanding General's (CG's) enlisted aide and cook. He has numerous tasks he must accomplish around the CG's quarters. Some unknowing people might make light of this sergeant's job. His role might seem unimportant compared to the Soldiers patrolling the streets of Baghdad, or climbing the steep mountains in Afghanistan, or those Emergency Ordinance Disposal Soldiers who respond to the call when bombs are found and need to be examined or disarmed.

The reality is, this Soldier has a key job. He is one of a small group of people who make sure the CG is ready and free to focus on leading our forces. He prepares the CG's food, he does tasks that allow the Commanding General to concentrate on the war. He even conducts dinners where the CG will meet and plan with other senior leaders. Because this Soldier does his job well, the CG doesn't have to worry about a hundred little extra details that would get him off the primary task of leading our Soldiers, Sailors, Airmen and Marines in combat operations.

In today's Bible verse, David assigned some men to guard the supplies, and then he honored them for their service. That is because he knew that in a successful team, everyone that is part of the team plays a key role and needs to be recognized for that role. Always strive to do the best you can no matter how small or great the task is. God expects nothing else and one day will reward His faithful servants.

While Jesus was still speaking, someone came from the house of
Jairus, the synagogue ruler. "Your daughter is dead," he said. "Don't
bother the teacher anymore."
Luke 8:49

My daughter likes to run and has been a member of the cross-country team at the two high schools she has attended. Currently, she is running in Texas. Due to the heat in the late summer and early fall the team runs in the morning before school. This past week the team and the school were struck by a tragedy when two of the girls on the team were hit by a truck as they were waiting in a designated median to finish crossing the street. The truck failed to make a full turn and came up over the median hitting the girls. One girl was killed, and the other girl was seriously hurt. The father of the girl who was killed is here in Iraq. I can only imagine his sorrow and pain as he was told of his daughter's death.

The story of Jairus' daughter and her death ended on a joyful note. Her life was restored when Jesus healed her. Jairus' daughter was twelve; the young girl killed in Texas was fourteen, and although she was not restored to physical life, she was restored spiritually. She had a wonderful trust and faith in Jesus. The death and loss of this precious child must hurt terribly for her father. As a Soldier in combat he may have been somewhat prepared for his own death, but not for the death of his daughter.

It is a comfort to know that her eternal life is secure and some beautiful day she and her family will be in the wonderful presence of God together. We have a glorious hope because of our faith in and relationship with Jesus. Faith and hope don't eliminate tragedy, but they do provide a true look to a brighter future.

He said to them, "Go into all the world and
preach the good news to all creation.
Mark 16:15

Today I flew with Lieutenant General Odierno, the Commanding General of Multi-National Corp-Iraq to visit an area just south of Baghdad. We stopped at several places, but by far the most interesting visit was to a combat outpost. These outposts are in places throughout the area that are in the midst of the Iraqi people. One thing that stands out is that these outposts are greatly different from the built-up, protected places from which most of our Soldiers conduct operations. There is a much higher level of risk at these combat outposts. We could sense the increased intensity and awareness among the Soldiers there.

That morning a truck with a machine gun mounted in the back had driven by, shooting at Soldiers in the outpost. I talked with several of the Soldiers at the outpost and they reported that getting shot at was a common occurrence. However, they also told me they liked their location and duty. Despite the more primitive conditions and danger that was a part of their daily life, they felt as if they were making a difference. What better way to impact the Iraqi people! The combat outpost is the place and format that allows us to reach out effectively to the populace and help them. It also puts us in a better position to engage the enemy operating in those areas and stop them from terrorizing the local citizens.

We must do the same thing in our spiritual lives. Staying in a secure, beautiful environment is nice, but it does not really put us in the place we need to be in order to reach those who are hurting, or to combat the action of evil and injustice we find in our local areas. God is calling us to go and find ways to share the good news with those who need it most.

Do nothing out of selfish ambition or vain conceit,
but in humility consider others above yourselves.
Philippians 2:3

One of the Army's stated values is selfless service. Nowhere is the concept of selfless service among men and women seen with greater clarity than here in combat. Every day we witness amazing accounts of selfless service. Recently, one of our great U.S. Soldiers was nominated for the nation's highest award, the Congressional Medal of Honor. He was nominated for covering a grenade with his body that had been thrown into his vehicle. His actions were focused on saving the other Soldiers in the vehicle, which he did at the cost of his own life.

A few weeks ago, one of our Religious Support Teams was in a vehicle that got hit with a roadside bomb. The chaplain was injured, and the chaplain assistant secured the chaplain, then he went back to the burning vehicle and helped pull the wounded gunner out of the vehicle before he could be hurt further.

These are powerful illustrations of selfless service; putting others ahead of yourself. Such selfless actions are also Christian expectations. Sometimes we hear the concept, "take care of yourself first," or "if you don't look out for yourself, no one else will." That is not what Jesus calls us to do. If we lived according to the Christian call, we would hear comments such as the following: "Those Christians are remarkable; they look out for the welfare of others as well as themselves." Jesus is our ultimate example, giving himself for all of humanity.

There is nothing wrong with placing the concerns and needs of others ahead of your own. God calls us to the high standard of service, humility, and considering the needs and welfare of others. Today, I challenge you to stop and purposely attempt to place someone else's needs before your own.

He said to Simon, "Put out into the deep water,
and let down the nets for a catch."
Simon answered, "Master, we've worked hard all night
and haven't caught anything.
But because You say so I will let down the nets."
When they had done so, they caught such a large number of fish that
their nets began to break. So they signaled their partners in the other
boat to come and help them.
And they came and filled both of the boats so full that they began to sink.
Luke 5:4-7

Whether it is our Soldiers, Sailors, Airmen, and Marines in Iraq or
Afghanistan; students attending junior or senior high school; or parents
trying to raise young children; there are always plenty of hardships and
obstacles to endure or overcome. All of us face hardship. All of us will
experience failure and loss at some point in life. How we react when
faced with the trials and hardships that abound in life is a key question
for every man or woman.

The Scripture reading for today records what constitutes a hardship
for millions of people every day; a bad day at work. Jesus used Peter's
boat to talk to the people who had gathered to hear Him. Then He tells
Peter and those with Him to put the boat out farther in the water and
re-cast their nets. They tell Jesus they have been fishing all night and
caught nothing, but they will follow His directions because He is the
Master. So they let down the nets, and they proceed to catch so many
fish that multiple boats can't hold all the catch.

These were professional fishermen, so they knew what they were doing,
but they had a bad day. It happens to everyone. For us here in combat, a
bad day often involves the death or serious wounding of Soldiers, so we
really want to avoid "bad" days. One way to avoid bad days or to better deal
with bad days is to listen to the voice of Jesus, and to follow the direction of
Jesus for our lives. Perhaps the Lord is calling you to try something again,
to recast your nets, or maybe He is calling you to follow Him for the very
first time. You can't go wrong by listening to the call of God.

And having been warned by God in a dream not to go back to Herod,
they returned to their own country by another route.
Matthew 2:12

As part of the Army Chief of Chaplain's visit to Iraq, we took him to the International Zone (IZ) in the middle of Baghdad. This is a relatively secure area of Baghdad, where the U.S. Embassy is located, as well as numerous Iraqi governmental offices. Entry into the IZ is tightly controlled and restricted, making the danger from direct small arms fire and improvised explosive devices fairly low. However, the threat from indirect fire, such as mortars and rockets launched from outside the IZ perimeter, continues to be a significant threat.

While the Chief of Chaplains was meeting with some senior leaders inside the embassy, a small group of us decided to wait outside the embassy under the shade of some palm trees. As we stood there, we suddenly heard a familiar but unwelcome sound. It was the whistle and rush of a rocket coming in toward our location. It was almost like slow motion as we heard the rocket coming in and pass just over our heads. The Sergeant Major from our section looked at me and said, "Uh-Oh," as we all dove to the ground. The round hit about 50 yards away and exploded. The attack was a pretty close call. It was enough to shake us up, but we all avoided injury.

Our Christian life often comes under attack, and although we don't hear an actual whistle, God has ways to warn us of impending dangers. The Magi were warned by a dream. The Holy Spirit will often warn us in our spirit if we are sensitive and listen. When we get that warning, we must act accordingly in order to avoid potential spiritual harm. God's word, the Bible, is the ultimate guide to avoid life's pitfalls. Be sure you are attentive to God's warnings in your life.

Take a few minutes to review the devotions you read during this past week. Write down three key lessons you learned. What aspect of the week's devotions resonates most with you? (If you are participating as a group or family take time to discuss these key lessons.)

_____

_____

_____

_____

Were there any aspects of the devotions that you had trouble identifying with? (If you are participating as a group or family take time to discuss the troubling portions.)

_____

_____

_____

_____

Write down names of people you know who might be struggling with some of the points from the devotions. Take time to pray for each person. (If you are participating as a group, or family take time to pray for the people identified.)

_____

_____

_____

_____

What changes do you feel God is calling you to make after reading last week's devotions? (If you are participating as a group or family take time to discuss those desired changes.)

_____

_____

_____

_____

Think about a personal example in your life that demonstrates the truth of the devotions. (If you are participating as a group or family take time to share some of the stories with each other.)

_____

_____

_____

_____

This is he who was spoken of through the prophet Isaiah:
"A voice of one calling in the desert, Prepare the way for the Lord,
make straight paths for him!"
Matthew 3:3 -

I was returning from Camp Anaconda where I had been visiting and conducting a staff-assistance visit with some of our great religious support teams that are deployed as part of the Multi-National Corps-Iraq. Once again, I was preparing to fly across Iraq. I and the others with me were taken out to our helicopter. As we sat with our backs against a protective concrete barrier, I watched the helicopter crew. They were all busy preparing the Blackhawk for its mission. The pilots were in the cockpit going over maps and checklists and making sure all the gauges were working. Other crew members were making sure all communication was up and functioning, checking batteries for the engine, and also making sure the anti-missile flare system was ready to go. The two crew members who operate the machine guns on each side of the helicopter, referred to as door-gunners, were carefully loading ammunition to make sure the guns would fire without jamming.

Later, we boarded the helicopter. As we prepared to take off, each person on the crew was busy with his own important tasks to make sure we got in the air safely, and stayed in the air for the duration of our flight. Each member of that crew had a job to do, and each task was essential in the overall effort.

I saw a great demonstration of how each member of a team is crucial to the overall success of a mission. As I thought about this, I reflected on our own need to prepare for our missions and calling in life, making sure we are equipped for success. Commit yourself to being the person you need to be on whatever team you belong: family, work, sports team, church, or volunteer organization.

This is love: not that we loved God, but that God loved us
and sent His Son as an atoning sacrifice for our sins.
1 John 4:10

While reading some material about sacrifice, I thought of the death of Jesus and the sacrifice God made for all of humanity. Later, I was sitting in our operations center during the Battle Update Assessment and once again I was struck by the reports of our Soldiers killed in battle and their sacrifice. It was a particularly bad day with several Soldiers killed and many others wounded by a suicide vehicle borne improvised explosive device (a bomb in a car). Other casualties were a result of direct and indirect fire. Yet, I know our brave Soldiers will continue to strive to bring security and freedom to Iraq and Afghanistan. Every day these men and women make great sacrifices to complete their missions, and sadly, some make the ultimate sacrifice with their lives.

General Douglas MacArthur said, *"The Soldier, above all other men, is required to perform the highest act of religious teaching – sacrifice. In battle and in the face of danger and death he discloses those divine attributes which his Maker gave when He created man in his own image. No physical courage and no brute instincts can take the place of the divine annunciation and spiritual uplift which will alone sustain him. However horrible the incident of war may be, the Soldier who is called upon to offer and to give his life for his country is the noblest development of mankind."*

I love and admire Soldiers. Today our women and men in uniform reflect the essence of MacArthur's words through their monumental sacrifices.

Jesus made an even greater sacrifice for all men and women. It was the most important sacrifice the world has ever known. He gave his life for all of humanity. Acknowledge and incorporate that sacrifice in your life today.

And do not forget to do good and to share with others,
for with such sacrifices God is pleased.
Hebrews 13:16

Yesterday I wrote about sacrifice. I don't want to too quickly pass on from the concept of sacrifice and move to the glory of the resurrection, which we will celebrate tomorrow on Easter Sunday.

The quote in yesterday's devotion by General Douglas MacArthur talked about a Soldier's duty in making sacrifices for his or her country and fellow Soldiers. Most every day we get reports of Soldiers who do exactly what MacArthur wrote about. Twice in the last six months, we have had brave warriors who have thrown their bodies over a grenade that was about to explode in the midst of other Soldiers or Marines. Their ultimate sacrifice no doubt saved lives of their fellow warriors. At least one of those heroes has been nominated to receive the Congressional Medal of Honor.

Additionally, we have Soldiers who place themselves between enemy fire and their friends or at times civilians who happen to be in the area. These men and women, who are here in Iraq and Afghanistan, far from the comfort and security of home, are sacrificing every day on behalf of our country and for the Iraqi people's freedom and justice.

Sacrifice is not a value or expectation meant only for Soldiers. The sacrifice of Jesus is the ultimate example for us as Christians. Throughout the Bible we see the mandate for us to sacrificially reach out and care for others. We are called to take the Good News of Jesus' love to the world, and it demands our sacrifice. Sacrifice is the bedrock foundation of reaching out to a hurting world. God is calling you to act with kindness and grace, and sacrificially share with others.

I applied my heart to what I observed and learned a lesson from what I saw.
Proverbs 24:32

Working dogs help us in a very large way in Iraq and Afghanistan. Dogs are especially helpful in sniffing out explosives. A handler and a dog will work at check-points and will often alert Soldiers that someone has a bomb or is trying to smuggle explosives into the country or into a city. The other night I was with a group of dogs and their handlers at a ceremony marking the successful completion of training that would help them perform their missions. Everyone at the ceremony seemed to love seeing and petting the dogs. I heard many comments from Soldiers who said how much they missed their dogs back in the United States. I thought it would be good to share a few things dogs might teach us, if we'd just take the time to learn from them. I know my dog has taught me all these lessons and more.

1. When someone you know comes home, run to say hello.
2. Take breaks and stretch a lot.
3. Allow people to hug you.
4. Often a simple growl will do. Only bite when necessary.
5. Stand up for those you love. Loyalty is a rare and valued treasure.
6. Enjoy the pleasure of a walk with a friend.
7. No matter how much trouble you get in, don't pout. Go back and be friends.
8. On blistering summer days, get a cool drink, and take a nap or relax in a cool place.
9. When someone you know is hurting, be quiet and just sit with her or him.
10. Don't be afraid to play, even when you're feeling old.

Do not be anxious about anything,
but in every situation, by prayer and petition,
with thanksgiving, present your requests to God.
Philippians 4:6

It has been a few days now, but the shock is still present for many Soldiers. Last week, in a surprise and unexpected announcement, the Secretary of Defense and the senior general of the military put the word out that active duty Soldiers now in Iraq and those to come for a while would serve fifteen months.

Previously the normal tour of duty for Army personnel was twelve months. The stress and toil on Soldiers being away from family and in a combat environment is very high. When you add one fourth of a year to that requirement, things can seem overwhelming. Most Soldiers are a little upset, but they take it in stride and continue on with their missions. No doubt the extension hurts, and it is an event that most would consider a bad circumstance.

All of us experience bad circumstances in our lives. What we do in the midst of bad situations is perhaps the critical element of our Christian witness. We are not called to show fake emotions and pretend that bad things don't happen. However, we should have a different bottom line. We have an eternal hope others don't. God tells us in Philippians not to be anxious, which at times can be difficult. Yet, despite the challenge, we are called to work at living anxiety free.

God may be saddened by circumstances we encounter, but it has not surprised or caught God off guard. You can take comfort that God knows where we are; God can use us wherever we are; God understands our feelings; God will be with us in any circumstance we encounter; and God can help us grow in any situation.

Give thanks that although there are times when we walk through the valley of the shadow of death, we are not stuck in that particular valley. God will bring us through.

In him and through faith in him we may approach God with
freedom and confidence.
Ephesians 3:12

I was flying in a helicopter with the Commanding General (CG) a
few days ago on the way to visit an infantry battalion in Northern Iraq.
Earlier that morning, just a few hours prior, terrorists destroyed an old,
historic bridge that spanned the Tigris River and connected East and
West portions of Baghdad. The CG wanted to see how much damage
had been done. We flew over Baghdad and circled the bridge that was
now in pieces and lying in the Tigris instead of over it. As I looked
out of the helicopter at the ruins below, I wondered why the terrorists
decided to blow up the bridge. It was a lifeline between the portions of
the city, and there are not a lot of bridges that cross the river.

The terrorists and insurgents just want to create chaos through
violence. They don't care whom they hurt or kill. They don't care
how much damage they do by destroying buildings, oil pipelines,
electric plants, or hospitals. They will do anything to undermine the
government.

I realized that they are dedicated to destroying bridges, and not just
bridges of concrete and metal. They want to destroy bridges between
the people of Iraq, bridges between Iraqis and the people of other
nations, bridges between different sects of the Islamic faith, and bridges
between the different tribal elements throughout the country.

As Christians our goal should be to build bridges. We must work
for people to come together and work together. The ultimate bridge is
Jesus. He serves as a bridge between humanity and a relationship with
God. Step out on the most secure bridge ever and find true freedom
and confidence in life.

All hard work brings a profit, but mere talk leads only to poverty.
Proverbs 14:23

I know your deeds, your hard work and your perseverance...
Revelation 2:2

My Dad's birthday was two days ago. I would have liked to be with him and be part of the celebration, but I knew that would not be possible since I was in Iraq. I did spend a few minutes reflecting about my Dad. I was blessed to have a father who was committed and dedicated to his family. I also observed this commitment in my Grandpa (my Dad's father). For both of them, this commitment was most demonstrated in their work ethic.

For most of my youth my Dad worked at American Machine and Foundry (AMF) and at the Empire-Detroit Steel plant in a city nearby our home town. My Grandpa worked most of his life on a farm that required lots of hours of work and was basically a 52-week-a-year commitment.

I'm sure there were days as I was growing up that my Dad or Grandpa were sick and did not go to work. Yet, I can't remember their ever not working. The only exception I remember is when Grandpa got badly burned and had to take time off from the farm, but only for a short time. Grandpa worked the farm into his 80's, and my Dad worked hard until his retirement from the steel mill. This same work ethic was instilled in me, my brother, and my sister. I started working on the farm at an early age. I had a paper route for several years, then I sold vegetables that I carried in big baskets door-to-door. Basically, I have worked in some manner since I was twelve or thirteen.

Work is a good thing, an honorable thing, and an activity that God wants us to have as a part of our lives. A good work ethic is part of our witness to God and will greatly contribute to a successful earthly life as well. Be a woman or man who is consistently seen as a hard and dependable worker.

Take a few minutes to review the devotions you read during this past week. Write down three key lessons you learned. What aspect of the week's devotions resonates most with you? (If you are participating as a group or family take time to discuss these key lessons.)

_____

_____

_____

_____

Were there any aspects of the devotions that you had trouble identifying with? (If you are participating as a group or family take time to discuss the troubling portions.)

_____

_____

_____

_____

Write down names of people you know who might be struggling with some of the points from the devotions. Take time to pray for each person. (If you are participating as a group, or family take time to pray for the people identified.)

_____

_____

_____

_____

What changes do you feel God is calling you to make after reading last week's devotions? (If you are participating as a group or family take time to discuss those desired changes.)

_____

_____

_____

_____

Think about a personal example in your life that demonstrates the truth of the devotions. (If you are participating as a group or family take time to share some of the stories with each other.)

_____

_____

_____

_____

Guard my life, for I am faithful to you;
save your servant who trusts in you. You are my God.
Psalm 86:2

Yesterday's reading dealt with commitment and the importance of work. With that in mind, I was struck by a quote I read years ago by William Booth, the founder of the Salvation Army. *"I will tell you the secret: God has had all that there was of me. There have been men with greater brains than I, even with greater opportunities, but from the day I got the poor of London on my heart and caught a vision of what Jesus Christ could do with me and them, on that day I made up my mind that God should have all of William Booth there was. And if there is anything of power in the Salvation Army, it is because God has had all the adoration of my heart, all the power of my will, and all the influence of my life."*

Sometimes we don't realize the impact and power we can have by simply giving a task or a goal everything we have. By working hard and diligently, we can accomplish great things. I see this philosophy put into action every day by our Soldiers. We have top-of-the-line equipment, the newest technology, and quality training. However, the big difference in our excellence is the day-to-day hard work and devotion to duty of our Soldiers giving their very best time after time.

We as Christians can also accomplish great things, just like the Soldiers in the Army or William Booth. We can do it by deciding to give all of ourselves to God and by declaring, "God, I trust in you, and I am devoted to you." Would it be that each of us could proclaim with the same resolve as Booth that God has all the adoration of my heart, all the power of my will, and all the influence of my life.

See to it that no one takes you captive
through hollow and deceptive philosophy,
which depends on human tradition and the basic principles of this world
rather than on Christ.
Colossians 2:8

I was out visiting the Religious Support Teams (RSTs) at Forward Operating Base (FOB) Warhorse and the surrounding area. One of the days, I flew to nearby FOB Normandy, where I met with two RSTs. It was a good trip, and as part of the visit, we went to some of the Soldier's living areas. I was told they were pretty bad at this FOB, and I wanted see and assess that for myself. As I went through the area and talked with some of the Soldiers and looked at their sleeping/living quarters, I realized how spartan it was. They had made some recent changes that made it more tolerable, but it was not the kind of place in which anyone would choose to live.

By contrast, as we left FOB Normandy and flew over the Diyala Province, I was struck by how beautiful and appealing it was when viewed from the air. As I looked out the doors of the helicopter, I saw a big, beautiful lake that stood out like a blue gem shimmering in the sunlight. There were green fields and numerous palm tree groves that gave the appearance of a wonderful, tranquil place. I could envision the possibility of a resort-type environment along the lake and the immediate vicinity.

The reality is much different. There is nothing tranquil about this region. Diyala is currently one of the more violent and deadly districts in Iraq. At FOB Warhorse the wall of heroes displays the name of every Soldier Killed in Action. There are far too many names on those walls, and the current unit has the most.

Satan is the great deceiver; he makes evil and wrong look good and enticing. Don't be fooled; see sin for what it is, and don't follow some hollow philosophy or teaching.

We continually remember before our God and Father your work produced by faith, your labor prompted by love, and your endurance inspired by hope in our Lord Jesus Christ.
1 Thessalonians 1:3

I was blessed to be invited to the ANZAC Day ceremony and celebration. You are probably asking, "What is ANZAC Day?" ANZAC stands for Australia, New Zealand Army Corp. ANZAC day has its roots in the efforts of a Task Force comprised of Australian and New Zealand military forces when they conducted the invasion of Gallipoli in 1915. Today ANZAC day was celebrated by Australians who hosted the event here in Iraq, and could probably best be described as a combination of the United States Memorial Day and Veteran's Day.

What an honor it was for me to be one of the few non-Australians at an early morning ceremony to start the ANZAC Day activities. The ceremony began just before dawn with "The lighting of the Sacred Flame." The flame, which flickered in an old historical receptacle just behind a stone monument, cast a somber light. The monument had the words, "Lest we Forget" carved into the stone. These words are from the repeating stanza in Kipling's famous Recessional which reads, "Lord God of Hosts, be with us yet, Lest we Forget, Lest we Forget."

The ceremony included an ANZAC Requiem read by a young Lieutenant from the Australian Army that gave more substance to those words. The following phrase was recited, *On this day, above all days, we recall those who served in war and who did not return..."*

God calls us to be grateful and remember those who have sacrificed for us. The greatest sacrifices are those that have brought the Freedom of Christ to others. Lest We Forget!

This is what the Lord Almighty said:
Administer true justice; show mercy and compassion to one another.
Zachariah 7:9

Not long ago a friend of mine who is with the Special Operations Forces that cover this region of Iraq stopped in to see me. He was passing through the Baghdad area and had a short amount of time between helicopter flights, so he dropped in for a visit. Like me, he is also a Ranger and we shared a few stories about when we were both at Fort Lewis in Washington and he was the Ranger Battalion Chaplain. That got me thinking about the Ranger Creed. The Creed records the essential elements of what it means to be a Ranger.

One portion of the Ranger Creed reads, *"Never shall I fail my comrades. I will always keep myself mentally alert, physically strong, and morally straight, and I will shoulder more than my share of the task, whatever it may be. One hundred percent and then some."* Rangers take the elements of the Creed seriously. Without doubt or question, Rangers are some of the most elite, feared, deadly, and dedicated Soldiers in the world.

Those of us who serve God would do well to have the same type of dedication and commitment to such principles. It would be good if we were known as men and women who could be counted on to support each other, *"Never shall we fail our comrades in the faith,"* or if we were known as people who always give one hundred percent or more, and were focused on keeping ourselves mentally alert, physically strong, and morally straight.

These are expected values for Christians. Are they part of your personal faith creed? They should be.

Let those who love the Lord hate evil,
for he guards the lives of his faithful ones
and delivers them from the hand of the wicked.
Psalm 97:10

Yesterday's devotion discussed some of the aspects of the Ranger Creed. There are additional elements that might also be applicable to us as Christians. The next part of the Creed I'd like to look at reads, ***"Energetically will I meet the enemies of my country. I shall defeat them on the field of battle for I am better trained and will fight with all my might. Surrender is not a Ranger word. I will never leave a fallen comrade to fall into the hands of the enemy, and under no circumstances will I ever embarrass my country."***

If you were to have a personal creed, it would not be the same as the Ranger Creed, but some of the ideas would likely be the same. The determination to stay true to your faith and never surrender would be a good example. Yes, at times living out God's principles can be hard but the idea of quitting or surrendering should not seriously be a part of our thought process. It goes beyond just not quitting; we are called to address the evil we encounter. The enemy of good and light must be confronted. God has given us the Holy Spirit to help us, and we are called to engage evil with all our might.

There is another big principle that Rangers have ingrained in their heart and head: ***"Never leave a fallen comrade."*** The balance between unwavering support and needed discipline is often difficult, especially since discipline can be a part of support. Work to find that balance, but perhaps more importantly, as we often say in the Army, make sure you've got the back of your friends. Fellow believers should especially feel secure that others of the church, of the faith, will not leave them to fight alone.

They came back to Moses and Aaron and the whole Israelite
community at Kadesh in the Desert of Paran. There they reported
to them and to the whole assembly and showed them the fruit of the
land... Then Caleb silenced the people before Moses and said, "We
should go up and take possession of the land, for we can certainly do it."
Numbers 13: 26 and 30

Sandstorms are frequent events in Iraq, and they can cause considerable problems. At times in the desert they can be so bad and violent that people can be seriously hurt if they cannot find cover. I've been in situations where the air is so thick with sand and dust that it is hard to breathe. There have been times I've had to stop, and even with my goggles on, still close my eyes for protection. In those times it was basically impossible to function effectively.

A group of Soldiers who were out on a mission were caught in one of these big sandstorms. When they realized the storm was closing in and appeared to be serious, they began to head for their base. As the wind blew harder and harder, the visibility grew worse and worse, until it was not safe to travel any farther. Because of the storm, the technological instruments they carried were rendered almost useless, and the Soldiers were not totally sure where they were.

They stopped, and as the sun set, they attempted to create some sort of security at their position. They spent a very anxiety-filled and miserable night. As the morning dawned, the storm had subsided. The Soldiers were shocked as they realized they were near their base; in fact, they could see the fence in the distance. The old saying of, "So close and yet so far away," was very true for them.

The Bible provides an account of when the people of Israel were very close to their goal of entering the Promised Land. They were hindered from reaching their goal; not by a storm, but by doubt and lack of trust in God.

Have you committed your life to Jesus? Don't just get close but still not secure. God loves you - give yourself to the love of Jesus.

And we know that in all things God works for the good of those who
love him, who have been called according to his purpose... What,
then, shall we say in response to these things? If God is for us, who
can be against us?
Romans 8: 28 and 31

Most Iraqis don't want a radical Islamic government. They want a
free Iraq and an Iraq that gives them choices about their lives without
fear of violence or death. Most of the Iraqi people are in favor of what
the coalition forces and the government of Iraq is trying to do for the
country. Yet, even with that said, we never really know exactly where
we stand with the Iraqi people. The question is often on the minds of
Soldiers, "Is this group or this individual really friendly or are we being
played?" We are never sure in this land of war and violence who is for
us and who is against us.

When I was a young boy growing up in Ohio, we had a big Buckeye
tree in our backyard. Almost every year a robin would build her nest
in that tree. I was always excited to discover that nest. It was so cool
to watch for those little eggs, and then wait for the birds to hatch from
their small blue-speckled shells. The baby robins had no feathers, big
bulging eyes, and gaping mouths. My Mom would make us stand back
from the tree once the young birds emerged, but I could still see their
little heads bobbing up and down, their mouths wide open, chirping
away and begging their mom for food.

Psalm 81:10 says, "I am the Lord your God...open your mouth
wide, and I will fill it." God's desire is to feed us. God longs to give us
spiritual food. God is for us.

Today I want you to know that God is for you. It is one of the key
points in the Romans 8 passage. You may not always be sure of others,
but you can be sure of God and know that God is for you.

Take a few minutes to review the devotions you read during this past week. Write down three key lessons you learned. What aspect of the week's devotions resonates most with you? (If you are participating as a group or family take time to discuss these key lessons.)

_____

_____

_____

_____

Were there any aspects of the devotions that you had trouble identifying with? (If you are participating as a group or family take time to discuss the troubling portions.)

_____

_____

_____

_____

Write down names of people you know who might be struggling with some of the points from the devotions. Take time to pray for each person. (If you are participating as a group, or family take time to pray for the people identified.)

_____

_____

_____

_____

What changes do you feel God is calling you to make after reading last week's devotions? (If you are participating as a group or family take time to discuss those desired changes.)

_____

_____

_____

_____

Think about a personal example in your life that demonstrates the truth of the devotions. (If you are participating as a group or family take time to share some of the stories with each other.)

_____

_____

_____

_____

The soothing tongue is a tree of life,
but a perverse tongue crushes the spirit.
Proverbs 15:4

This war is not just limited to the physical violence. The war of words and the war of the pen is also raging. Muqtada al-Sadr, the radical Shiite Islamic cleric, regularly spouts rhetoric of violence and anarchy, causing more death and heartache. From the home-front it is often demoralizing to read or watch media accounts of the war in Iraq from papers or TV shows in the United States. People seem to get so angry and say things that are horrible and untrue.

Someone sent a story to me about a young boy with a bad temper who would say mean and unkind things when he was angry. His father gave him a bag of nails and told him that every time he lost his temper, he should hammer a nail in the back fence. The first couple of days the boy drove a whole bunch of nails into the fence. Then the number began to decrease. He discovered it was easier to hold his temper than to drive the nails into the fence.

Finally, the boy got to the point that he was not losing his temper. He told his father about it, and the father suggested the boy now pull out one nail for each day he was able to hold his temper. The days passed, and finally, the young boy was able to tell his dad that all the nails were gone.

The father took his son by the hand and led him to the fence. "You have done well son, but look at the holes in the fence. The fence will never be the same. When you say things in anger, they leave scars, just like these holes in the fence."

It is good and right to apologize when we hurt someone, but the wound is still there. Often a verbal wound can be just as bad as a physical one. God calls us to be kind and watch what we say.

Now when Daniel learned that the decree had been published, he went home to his upstairs room where the windows opened toward Jerusalem. Three times a day he got down on his knees and prayed, giving thanks to his God, just as he had done before.

Daniel 6:10

I was invited to speak at a National Day of Prayer luncheon in the Multi-National Division-North area of operations. I knew that the two-star commanding general of the division would be in attendance, as well as other leaders from the division. I wanted to speak about the importance and power of prayer, as well as address some leadership principles from a Biblical perspective. (I know I've used this same Scripture before, but there are so many valuable lessons in this story)

I chose the Bible story of Daniel and the lion's den. Daniel is on the verge of being made second in command by the King, and the other leaders are not happy with that course of action. They go to the King and lie to him and convince him to make a decree that no one can pray to anyone but the King. They wanted to corner Daniel and bring him down. Since they could not find anything in Daniel's life that was wrong, they decided to set a trap for him. They knew he was a man of faith, and they knew he would continue to pray to God despite the King's decree.

Sure enough, the Bible tells us that as soon as Daniel learned of the King's decree, he went to his room and prayed. This is exactly what those opposing Daniel knew he would do.

How I wish that I and other believers would pray as our first reaction when we smell the smoke or feel the flames of discontent or problems. Daniel understood what his first response needed to be, and it was a habit for him. Develop a routine of going to God in prayer whether in good times or bad. Cultivate a Daniel-type reputation.

Then they said to the king, "Daniel, who is one of the exiles from Judah, pays no attention to you, O king, or to the decree you put in writing. He still prays three times a day." When the king heard this, he was greatly distressed...

Daniel 6: 13-14a

Yesterday the devotion was based on the story of Daniel and the lions' den and the need to be people of prayer. The story has other key lessons for the men and women of God to incorporate in their lives.

The king made a decree that he issued based on an incomplete picture he was presented by some his subordinate leaders. They told him everyone wanted the decree, but that was not true. The other leaders had purposely left Daniel out of the process. So, the king made a foolish decision. He should have been more careful about using his authority. Our words, spoken or written, can have great consequences. Be careful about what you say or promise; your tongue is a powerful tool.

The king was presented with a big problem due to the situation caused by the decree and Daniel's action. Daniel had violated his decree. Yes, the decree of the king was a big deal. The story is clear about the king's reaction. He was distressed and unhappy about having to punish Daniel. The king knew Daniel was a good person, but he felt obligated because of the decree he had made. The law of the land made it extremely important to hold fast to decrees made by the king.

However, when you are the "king/queen" (the leader), be the king/queen and lead. If you make a bad a decision, don't compound it by continuing down a foolish path that you know is wrong. When you know you have made a bad decision, you need to stop, admit your error or mistake, and head down the right path.

God is calling each of us to be men and women of integrity and courage despite the risk or cost. Decide today that you will strive to be a person who is known for doing what is right in God's eyes.

Your word is a lamp for my feet and a light on my path.
Psalm 119:105 -

I was out running on the roads around our base a little earlier than usual. I normally go out the door of my containerized housing unit to do fitness training around 5:15 a.m., but today I was out at 4:30 a.m. The heat is already creeping up to near 110 degrees during the day, and the early morning is the best time to go out and run. When I first started running around the camp, I would often see jackals in the early morning. I did not really see the jackals' body, just the eyes glowing in the darkness. It is pretty creepy. I have not seen any jackals for a couple months now. I'm hoping the animal management folks have been able to get them under control.

When there is a bright, full moon out in the morning, it casts a glow that actually allows me to see where I am going with no problems. However, on those mornings when there is not much moon light it can be very dark out as I run through areas of the camp. In order to see on those dark mornings I have a small light that is attached to a band that goes around my head. It casts a good, strong beam of light that lands right in front of me. The light allows me to see where my feet are getting ready to strike the ground. It enables me to see the road and avoid holes, rocks, and other obstacles that might cause me to fall or stumble. It also makes me feel safer about seeing animals that might be out on the road or paths.

God's Word is referred to as, *"a lamp for my feet and a light for my path."* Understanding the direction and guidance of God through His Word enables us to identify many obstacles in life. If we incorporate the guidance, it can keep us from falling and stumbling in our daily life. Make sure you devote regular time to read God's word so that you can better see your way through life.

For you, Lord, have delivered my soul from death, my eyes from
tears, my feet from stumbling, that I may
walk before the Lord in the land of the living.
Psalm 116:8-9

Loneliness and fear can influence men and women to do some rather dumb things. Both of those elements are a constant challenge for the Soldiers here in Iraq. The young men and women serving in Afghanistan and Iraq as part of the U.S. military have all been uprooted from their families and closest friends. Despite the fact that it is hard for Soldiers to actually be alone in this environment, they nevertheless get lonely. The bravery of most of our Soldiers is unquestioned, and the majority of our young warriors demonstrate valor and courage every day. That demonstration of valor and courage does not mean they are not without fear. Afghanistan and Iraq are often dangerous and violent places. All those factors and more can make it very tough to, *"walk before the Lord in the land of the living."*

As difficult as walking before the Lord in the land of the living may be, God is call us to do just that. Walking before God in the land of the living means serving God where you are. It may not be the place you'd like to be or feel comfortable being, but as long as you are there, you are called to serve God and to live each day for Jesus.

Your situation may be very difficult, just like our Soldiers in combat. Determine in your heart and mind to be true and faithful to God. Don't look for comfort in the arms of another person, or in a bad or wrong internet site, or in a bottle or some drug, or in violence to your spouse, children or others. Be faithful to God who can uphold you with a strong and abiding love. A faithful walk with God won't eliminate times of trouble, but it will help those trials and troubles seem less burdensome and help you cope in the best ways possible.

She speaks with wisdom, and faithful instruction is on her tongue. She watches over the affairs of her household and does not eat the bread of idleness. Her children arise and call her blessed; her husband also, and he praises her: "Many women do noble things, but you surpass them all." Charm is deceptive, and beauty is fleeting; but a woman who fears the Lord is to be praised. Give her the reward she has earned, and let her works bring her praise at the city gate.
Proverbs 31: 26-31

I'm writing this on Mother's Day. I am so grateful for my Mom. Not many people who had a truly loving Mother look back in their life and fail to realize what a blessing their Moms were to them. Our Mothers deserve to be honored for their love and faithful service to families. Moms are called on to persevere and provide in all sorts of situations. What follows today and tomorrow is a tribute to all those Moms.

This tribute is for all the Moms who have sat up all night with sick toddlers in their arms, wiping up vomit laced with Goldfish crackers and juice from a little plastic box, and saying, "It's okay, Mommy is here." It is for all the Moms who have watched their sons and daughters go off to war and cried long after they were gone. It is for reading *Are you my Mother*" twice a night for weeks straight, then reading it again a few weeks later. It is for all the Moms who struggle; who yell at their kids in the grocery store and then give them a good swat on the bottom. It is for all the Moms who don't know what to say when their 15-year-old daughter comes home with a belly-button ring. It is for all the Moms who taught their children to tie their shoe laces before they started school and also for those who opted for Velcro instead. It is for all the Moms who gave birth to babies they will never see, and the Moms who adopted those babies and gave them good homes in which to live and grow up in.

"God, we thank you for our Moms, those living and those who have gone to be with you. They are a true blessing and deserve all the praise we can give."

She gets up while it is still dark; she provides food for her family
and portions for her servant girls. She considers a field and buys it;
out of her earnings she plants a vineyard. She sets about her work
vigorously; her arms are strong for her tasks.
She sees that her trading is profitable,
and her lamp does not go out at night.
In her hand she holds the distaff and grasps the spindle with her fingers.
She opens her arms to the poor and extends her hands to the needy.
Proverbs 31:15-20

I thought the tribute to Mothers deserved two days. Actually, my
Mom and my wife and all other Moms deserve much more than that.
Thank your Mom again today and remember all the things she has
done for you and your family as you read this.

This is for all the Moms of the victims of Columbine, Virginia
Tech, and other tragic murders. This is for the Moms of survivors, and
the Moms who watch their TVs in horror, hugging their child who just
came home from school, safely. This is for all the Moms here in Iraq or
Afghanistan, serving their nation and unable to be with the children
they love; who cry each night as they say a prayer for their sons and
daughters. This is for all the Moms who run carpools and make cookies
and sew Halloween costumes, and all the Moms who don't. This is for
all the Moms that sat down with their children and explained all about
making babies, and those who wanted to but couldn't. This is for all the
Moms who show up at work with spit-up in their hair and milk or juice
stains on their blouses. This is for all the Moms who teach their sons
how to cook and daughters to throw a ball or sink a jump shot. This
is for all the Moms who sent their child to school with a stomachache,
ear-ache, or sore throat, assuring them they'd be just fine, only to get
a call from the school to pick them because they threw-up or the ear
drum broke. This is for all the young Moms stumbling through diaper
changes and sleep deprivation, and the mature Moms learning to let go.

This is for all Moms. Thank you and God Bless You!

Take a few minutes to review the devotions you read during this past week. Write down three key lessons you learned. What aspect of the week's devotions resonates most with you? (If you are participating as a group or family take time to discuss these key lessons.)

_____

_____

_____

_____

Were there any aspects of the devotions that you had trouble identifying with? (If you are participating as a group or family take time to discuss the troubling portions.)

_____

_____

_____

_____

Write down names of people you know who might be struggling with some of the points from the devotions. Take time to pray for each person. (If you are participating as a group, or family take time to pray for the people identified.)

_____

_____

_____

_____

What changes do you feel God is calling you to make after reading last week's devotions? (If you are participating as a group or family take time to discuss those desired changes.)

_____

_____

_____

_____

Think about a personal example in your life that demonstrates the truth of the devotions. (If you are participating as a group or family take time to share some of the stories with each other.)

_____

_____

_____

_____

Pride goes before destruction, a haughty spirit before a fall.
Proverbs 16:18

Soldiers are an interesting group of people, loyal to each other, dedicated to their missions, and proud of what they do for the nation. Yet, it is a pride that is tempered with reality, knowing that if they get too puffed up and fail to stay focused, they can quickly find themselves in a dangerous fall.

There is an old story that illustrates this concept. A frog wanted to get out of his cold winter climate. Some of the local geese said he should come with them as they migrated. Of course the frog could not fly, so he came up with an idea for the problem. "I'm so smart," he said. He asked two geese to each pick up the end of a stick. The frog could hold on to the stick with his mouth. Soon the frog and the geese began their journey. As they flew over a playground, the children looked up to stare at the amazing sight. One of the children said, "Who would have thought of such a brilliant plan?" The frog was so full of his own importance that he cried out, "It was my idea!" His pride was his undoing. As soon as he opened his mouth, he let go of the stick and fell to his death.

It is good to have a positive self-image and be aware of the actions we are involved with that exceed expectations. However, we must not become too full of ourselves and think we are so important that we have it all together.

It will always serve us well to remember and acknowledge that all gifts come from our creator, God almighty. C.S. Lewis said, "Humility is not thinking less of yourself but thinking of yourself less." Great words to live by. Strive each day to live with a true spirit of humility.

Your words have supported those who stumbled; you have
strengthened faltering knees.
Job 4:4

A difficult task. Defining what makes a task difficult is not always easy. However, I can definitely say that one of the most difficult tasks the chaplains face in combat is planning and conducting memorial ceremonies for the Soldiers who are killed in action. The ceremonies are not difficult in terms of the actual organization, set-up, and conduct of the event. The difficulty is a result of intangible elements. Some aspects of what we do can't be measured or are hard to measure, because the impact is primarily on the emotional, mental, and spiritual welfare of those involved. Sadly, our Religious Support Teams have conducted hundreds of memorial ceremonies for Soldiers, Sailors, Airmen, and Marines who have died in service to the nation. They have also visited and ministered to thousands of wounded in action.

Sometimes what makes the task difficult for fellow Soldiers is unfinished "business" or a sense of incompleteness. Maybe they had not told a team member just how important he or she was to the person. Perhaps there were some words or actions left unsaid or undone, or maybe they wanted to offer some words of encouragement but had not done so, and now the friend/co-worker is dead. Sadly, from time to time, there is an unresolved negative event that haunts the remaining person.

Today is a good day to express your care, love, or respect for someone in your life. Choose to be an upholder and encourager, or maybe you need to forgive someone. Your words may be the exact thing someone needs to keep from faltering and find success. It may also begin a healing process in you that has caused you to be bitter, angry, or sad. Now is the time to begin the process of renewal.

The Lord is my light and my salvation-- whom shall I fear?
The Lord is the stronghold of my life-- of whom shall I be afraid?
Psalm 27:1

A little over a week ago, the devotion was about my own experience of finding God's peace when fear was trying to overwhelm me. Fear is an insidious emotion. It can cause us to stop our involvement in critical or even routine tasks, frozen like an animal caught in the bright lights of an approaching car. Fear can cause people who are normally even-tempered to lose control and lash out with a great amount of anger. It is important that we don't allow fear to rule us.

A chaplain at one of our Forward Operating Bases told me about a recent event. A Soldier who was a gunner on a Humvee (High Mobility Multipurpose Wheeled Vehicle) came under attack with the rest of his vehicle crew. The Humvee was hit by multiple IEDs, and the gas tank ruptured after being struck by shrapnel. The vehicle caught on fire, and there were flames inside. One person died and two others were burned, including the gunner who had minor burns. As the days went on, he found himself shaking and fearful. He went to the Combat Stress Control Team (mental health folks), who provide great help for many people, but he did not find much relief there or advice he felt comfortable with. He also sought out the medical providers at his location, who do such wonderful and heroic work. But he did not find that the help offered was sufficient or realistic.

Then he turned to his chaplain who told him about his father who had been similarly effected in WWII until he prayed for God's help and deliverance. The Soldier did the same and found his fear removed. Are you fearful today? Ask God for strength and courage.

I counsel you to buy from me gold refined in the fire,
so you can become rich;
and white clothes to wear, so you can cover your shameful nakedness;
and salve to put on your eyes, so you can see.
Revelation 3:18

One of the unique things about being in another country, in a very different culture than the U.S., is experiencing and meeting some of the people from the host nation or local region. I don't get to meet a whole lot of Iraqis, but I have met a few, and talking with one helped open my eyes to reality. This man converted to Christianity about three years ago, and it has resulted in his complete rejection by his parents and his brothers and sisters, to the point where they now consider him dead. As far as they are concerned, he no longer exists as a real person. He has had to contend with being bombed, shot at, and frequently threatened for his faith in Jesus. At one point his daughter was killed in one of the bombings.

He reads about the U.S. and our freedom to worship as we choose, as well as other aspects of American life. He wonders why we as citizens of such a great country would fail to be more thankful for what we have and so prone to complain about what we have or don't have. He asks why we waste so much of what we have: food, space, time, and other personal goods. He was very perplexed about what he perceived as our children's lack of respect for parents and elders, and he laughed about an article he read that talked about a drive-in church located in California. He thought it was a joke and could not understand why people would want to attend church in their cars.

The book of Revelation provides a lesson about the spiritual danger of not seeing yourself as you really are. Have you taken an honest look at your life, or do you need to ask God to open your eyes?

From that day on, half of my men did the work, while the other half
were equipped with spears, shields, bows and armor. The officers
posted themselves behind all the people of Judah who were building
the wall. Those who carried materials
did their work with one hand and held a weapon in the other.
Nehemiah 4:16-17

Soldiers in combat must always be ready to defend themselves. I
was especially aware of this when I visited a Joint Security Station (JSS)
in a volatile area of Baghdad. These JSSs have been set-up all over Iraq,
but the primary effort is in the Baghdad area of operations. The hope
and commitment is to have these stations, which are jointly operated
by Iraqi and U.S. forces, in areas where there has been a lack of security
and a high level of violence and injustice. The intention is that these
JSSs will help decrease the violence and create a safer environment.

The Soldiers at these stations circulate throughout the area of the
city where they are located. They reach out to the local populace and
most of the time provide a calm and secure presence. However, there are
also many times when they come under attack from different groups,
with numerous types of weapons, and from various directions. At those
times they must be ready. There is no time to run and find a weapon or
the ammo for the weapon; no time to conduct routine maintenance or
clean the weapon; no time to run across the compound to grab a helmet
or put on your protective gear. Readiness is a watchword of the Soldier.

The men who stood shoulder-to-shoulder with Nehemiah were
much the same. While they worked, they also remained ready to fight
the enemy with their weapons in their hands. The spiritual lesson is
clear for those of us who serve God. We must be "Soldiers of God,"
ready to engage the enemy when evil and injustice are made evident
or provide support to those who are weary and are in need of a strong
helping hand. Are you ready?

Woe to those who call evil good and good evil,
who put darkness for light and light for darkness,
who put bitter for sweet and sweet for bitter.
Isaiah 5:20

It is amazing to listen to some of the rhetoric and posturing offered by al-Qaeda; a mostly Sunni Iraq organization with foreign leadership and direction that is dedicated to causing chaos and confusion through violence. The reality is they want control and power, and they are willing to go to any length or extreme to get either of them. Therefore, they conduct bombings of mosques and other Islamic holy sites; they use vehicles with large amounts of explosives to blow up bridges, markets filled with civilians, or even sites with children. They kidnap, torture, and murder men and women whose only "crime" is not to believe the same as those in al-Qaeda. It is not the action they take that amazes me, although I admit the cruelty and violence are horrid. The amazing part is that they believe their actions are justified. They have fooled themselves, but hopefully not too many others, into calling evil good and good evil. They have replaced light with darkness.

As much as this should sicken us, we should be careful not to point our fingers too quickly. This is an age-old problem. In the time of Isaiah, the people of God did the same thing, making evil seem okay and failing to uphold high values, morals, and virtue. Today we do the same thing in many ways. Our political leaders accept donations to further agendas they know are wrong. We make heroes of men and women who at best do no real good and at worst are morally bankrupt.

Others will try to convince you that evil is good or good is evil. Don't act contrary to what you know is correct. Stand strong for what God tells us is good and right, and don't give into societal pressure to call evil good or wrong right.

Rescue me, Lord, from evildoers; protect me from the violent,
who devise evil plans in their hearts and stir up war every day.
Psalm 140: 1-2

Sometimes the reports we get at headquarters seem to catch our attention in an extraordinary way. Today we got a report about a patrol that was hit by an improvised explosive device. This bomb, emplaced under the road, was extremely powerful and caused one of our heavy-armored vehicles to flip over and catch fire. Five of our Soldiers were killed in the attack. Then as the medical and rescue teams responded, they too came under attack. The chaplain who was in one of the responding Humvees was wounded. He was not seriously hurt and was quickly back to work, providing ministry to his Soldiers.

This very same day I read Psalms 138-141. Psalm 138 states, *"Though I walk in the midst of trouble, you preserve my life: you stretch out your hand against the anger of my foes, with your right hand you save me."* Psalm 140 begins, *"Rescue me from evildoers; protect me from the violent, who devise evil plans in their hearts and stir up war every day."*

Men and women with evil intentions were found in the Old Testament times and we continue to find such people today as well. They often cause great pain and heartache to those who are touched by their evil plans and ways. The good thing is that God will not let them get away with their horrific acts. Eventually, they will be held accountable on the eternal scale of justice.

God is faithful, so keep your eyes on him even in the midst of pain and suffering, and your faith will be rewarded. We serve a mighty God who loves and cares for us. He will rescue His children.

Take a few minutes to review the devotions you read during this past week. Write down three key lessons you learned. What aspect of the week's devotions resonates most with you? (If you are participating as a group or family take time to discuss these key lessons.)

_____

_____

_____

_____

Were there any aspects of the devotions that you had trouble identifying with? (If you are participating as a group or family take time to discuss the troubling portions.)

_____

_____

_____

_____

Write down names of people you know who might be struggling with some of the points from the devotions. Take time to pray for each person. (If you are participating as a group, or family take time to pray for the people identified.)

_____

_____

_____

_____

What changes do you feel God is calling you to make after reading last week's devotions? (If you are participating as a group or family take time to discuss those desired changes.)

_____

_____

_____

_____

Think about a personal example in your life that demonstrates the truth of the devotions. (If you are participating as a group or family take time to share some of the stories with each other.)

_____

_____

_____

_____

Chaplain Tarvin took this picture while flying over Baghdad, Iraq.
(he is in another helicopter headed for a Forward Operating Base)

Chaplain Tarvin presents Mac Powell, lead singer of Third Day,
with a Thank You gift.

Chaplain Tarvin on the right and Chaplain Outen on the left prior to heading out on a convoy in the Samarra region of Iraq.

Chaplain Tarvin in front of his temporary living quarters at Forward Operating Base Brassfield-Mora.

Chaplain Tarvin traveled extensively throughout Iraq. Here he is getting ready for some Blackhawk helicopter time.

Chaplain Tarvin at a Special Forces Medical Clinic in Iraq. The clinic delivered medical care for the local community. The Unit Ministry Team provided needed items for women and children at the clinic.

Chaplain Tarvin at Saint Elijah's. An ancient Assyrian Christian monastery near Mosul, Iraq. Constructed by Assyrian Monks in the sixth century and later operated by the Chaldean order. In 1743 the Monks were given an ultimatum by Persian invaders and up to 150 of the Monks were massacred when they refused to leave.

I am not saying this because I am in need,
for I have learned to be content whatever the circumstances.
Philippians 4:11

Contentment, happiness, joyfulness - how do you get to these states? There are many things that bring me joy and happiness: A long, quiet run through wooded paths; sleeping in on a cold, rainy morning; eating out at a nice restaurant with my wife; riding my Harley on a winding country road; or just spending some time with my daughters. For Soldiers who are fighting a cruel and evil enemy in 120 plus degree heat and without the comforts most people take for granted, those type of events that I listed above are mostly dreams of a time in the future. A Soldier quickly learns that along with the happy times come times of hurt and pain. No one truly likes the hard times, but hard times do serve many purposes.

It is most often through the times of strife and difficulty that significant gains are made. Also, we are frequently able to distinguish that it is in the trials and difficult times of life that the true source of happiness and contentment is recognized. That source is Jesus. Jesus is the one who gives ultimate meaning to the other things that make us "happy" and to life in general.

I find Paul's ability to find contentment in any situation a comforting thought. This comes from a man who was constantly being pressured and abused. Many times his ability to live contentedly had to be a strong, intractable, positive decision. As trials raged around him, he chose to be happy, to be joyful and to be content. Paul's choices caused him to learn the sufficiency of a relationship with Jesus.

Determine that today you will strive to be content in all situations, with the full realization that with Jesus in your life, contentment is possible.

Do not be overcome by evil, but overcome evil with good.
Romans 12:21

The presence, influence, and actual working of evil are evident in Afghanistan and Iraq. Yet, that aspect of life in Afghanistan and Iraq is not that much different than the city, state, or country you live in today. Evil is everywhere, and a good question to ask yourself is, "How do I overcome evil?"

The answer is found in the Bible. Paul tells the believers in Rome not to be overcome by evil, but to overcome the evil with good. How do we do that? The next few devotions will address that question, because no matter where we are in the world, no matter what we are doing, evil will be a constant threat, and we are called to overcome it.

The first thing we must do to overcome evil is found in an assumption Paul makes. To whom is Paul writing this letter? The letter is written to believers, those men and women who have placed their lives in the hands of God through Jesus Christ. There are people in the world who still carry out the practice of nailing items on their door to keep evil away: hawk feathers to keep one kind of evil away, eagle feathers to keep another type away, animal skins or other animal parts to keep other types of evil away.

As Christians we are just as interested in keeping evil away, but we know that charms or totems are not the answer. The answer of how to keep evil away has multiple aspects to it, and the first aspect is a reliance on Jesus as our Lord. Do you want to overcome evil in your life? The first and most important step in doing that is trusting God with your life.

And lead us not into temptation, but deliver us from the evil one.
Matthew 6:13

Overcoming evil was the topic yesterday and will be the theme for a few days. It is a task we are all faced with, so it does us good to understand how we can best go about that task. Our first step is to place ourselves in God's hand. The second step to overcome evil is to be a person of prayer. Matthew 6:9-13 records Jesus' instructions on how to pray, and verse thirteen says ask to, "be delivered from evil or the evil one." There is an enemy out there who wants to tear you down, who wants to influence you in a negative way. If we really want to overcome evil, we need to ask God to keep us out of evil's grasp, out of the clutches of satan.

There is another aspect of overcoming evil that goes hand-in-hand with the above concept. I'd classify it as common sense, but of course we often fail to use our common sense. In this case 1 Thessalonians 5:22 is the verse that guides us to, "avoid every kind of evil." It makes sense that if you do not want to have bad and evil come your way, then stay away from it, avoid it. Most of us, especially Soldiers, seem to have a propensity to think we are strong and can overcome any situation. God knows better, so He tells us to stay away from evil. Being around evil or bad habits has a tendency to drag us down.

Participation or just being too close to sin can be fatefully bad. Too many believers want to be cool, popular, and accepted at the expense of being too near the flame and getting burned. God says pray and stay away. Pray to overcome evil and to be victorious in defeating evil when it comes your way. Perhaps more importantly, stay away from evil and those things you know will tempt you.

Love must be sincere. Hate what is evil; cling to what is good.
Romans12:9

So far the pathway to overcoming evil includes the need to make sure we are serving God, that we are a people who make overcoming evil in our lives a part of our prayers, and that we try to avoid evil if we can. God tells us that there is another key aspect to overcoming evil. We are called to hate what is evil. Many people don't like to use such a strong term. Should we really hate anything? Yes, we should. Verse nine of Romans 12 reads, "Hate what is evil." When we are walking with God, when we are in a right relationship with God, we should hate evil. We should feel a revulsion about the sin we encounter. However, we must be careful not to confuse the sin with the sinner. God tells us to hate the sin but not the sinner. We are all sinners and have fallen short of God's expectation. The fact is, we are called to love the sinner, but at the same time hate the sin. Developing and implementing ways to communicate and make clear this mandate to hate the sin (evil) but love the sinner is a difficult task.

Many folks get caught in this dilemma and decide on one of two wrong actions. They decide to accept both the sin and sinner, which is wrong. To some people it may appear to be a loving action, but in the long run it is harmful to the persons directly involved and to humanity in general. The other course of action is also way off course, and that is the decision to hate both the sin and the sinner. This is definitely contrary to God's design and desire.

So, as difficult as it is, we must hate the evil we encounter, but at the same time strive to demonstrate a love of the person caught in sin's destructive grip.

Love must be sincere. Hate what is evil; cling to what is good.
Romans 12:9

Soldiers are not alone in the mission to overcome evil. It is a problem or issue that confronts all of us. There are numerous aspects to any effort in combating and overcoming evil. Over the last few devotions, we have identified that the ability to overcome evil has its foundation on a firm relationship with Jesus. Also key in the effort is spending time in prayer and asking God to keep us from evil. A third aspect of overcoming evil is our own personal efforts to avoid evil in our life. Yesterday, we added a fourth element in our battle against evil and that is our call to hate evil. Romans 12:9 specifically mandates that attitude, but there is a second part of that verse that tells us to cling to what is good.

A picture of a Soldier and a child demonstrated this principle for me. The picture was taken shortly after a bomb, planted by al-Qaeda insurgents, exploded in a market area of Baghdad. The bomb caused a large amount of damage, killed eight people, and wounded many more. In the midst of the chaos and violence, our Soldiers arrived to provide help and care. One Soldier found a toddler in the rubble. The child was alone, scared, and bleeding from numerous cuts. The Soldier tenderly picked the child up, gently embracing and speaking kindly to the child. The little boy wrapped his arms around the Soldier and would not let go, recognizing the Soldier as good. The child was clinging to good.

We need to determine the good of God in our life and cling to it as that child clung to the Soldier. Embrace God and adhere to the good in life; hold on to what you know is good and right for all you are worth.

The Spirit you received does not make you slaves, so that you live
in fear again; rather, the Spirit you received brought about your
adoption. And by him we cry, "Abba, Father."
Romans 8:15

The last two devotions were based on a verse from the book of
Romans and so is today's devotion. A young Soldier said that before he
was told about Jesus and committed his life to serving Him, he used
to regularly visit a tarot card reader as well as a fortune teller. He said
he had a great fear of the future and wanted some glimpse of what was
ahead and hopefully a greater sense of security.

After he was walking with Jesus, some fellow Soldiers in a Bible
study let him know that he need not fear the future and that the fortune
tellers and card readers did not offer any true security or insight. True
insight and security would only be found in his relationship with Jesus.
As this Soldier grew in his relationship with Jesus, he was able to take
great comfort in this security.

As Americans, we celebrate the freedom of our nation every July
Fourth. Freedom is a wonderful blessing that we enjoy in the United
States. It is one of the things we are hoping to win for the people of
Afghanistan and Iraq; freedom to have a voice in their government,
freedom to live without fear of death or torture based on how they
choose to live or believe, and other freedoms we often take for granted.

I hope and pray the people of Iraq and Afghanistan get this
freedom, but I've come to see even more clearly than before that they
need the true freedom that comes through Christ. Without Jesus there
is never true freedom. Ask yourself today, "Am I truly free?" That
answer can only be affirmed if you have given your heart to God by
accepting Jesus as your Lord and Savior.

Consequently, you are no longer foreigners and strangers, but fellow citizens with God's people and members of God's household, built on the foundation of the apostles and prophets, with Christ Jesus himself as the chief cornerstone.
Ephesians 2:19-20

Yesterday a special ceremony was held here at Camp Victory, Iraq. The ceremony was a combination of two fantastic events, and I was honored to open the entire proceedings with a prayer. We were celebrating The Fourth of July and the other event was a Naturalization Ceremony. Over one hundred and sixty of our Soldiers, Sailors, Airmen, and Marines who are here fighting for our country were sworn in as United States' citizens. I have attended naturalization ceremonies before, and it is amazing how proud and honored the men and women who take part are about becoming Americans. It goes way beyond the desire for certain rights or blessings they might obtain from citizenship. Their pride and sense of honor is based on being part of a larger dream, of being part of a people who enjoy an unprecedented freedom and who offer a hope that goes beyond self-interest, and extends to people throughout the world.

As wonderful as citizenship in the United States is, men and women who have made a commitment to Jesus are now citizens of an even greater place. Followers of Christ are citizens of God's Kingdom. As discussed in yesterday's devotion, freedom is a wonderful and precious thing. It is of such great value that humanity is willing to fight for it. But there is a greater more important citizenship and subsequent freedom that comes from accepting and serving Jesus. How wonderful to know that our citizenship is in heaven and that our freedom and hope are truly beyond measure.

Take a few minutes to review the devotions you read during this past week. Write down three key lessons you learned. What aspect of the week's devotions resonates most with you? (If you are participating as a group or family take time to discuss these key lessons.)

_____

_____

_____

_____

Were there any aspects of the devotions that you had trouble identifying with? (If you are participating as a group or family take time to discuss the troubling portions.)

_____

_____

_____

_____

Write down names of people you know who might be struggling with some of the points from the devotions. Take time to pray for each person. (If you are participating as a group, or family take time to pray for the people identified.)

_____

_____

_____

_____

What changes do you feel God is calling you to make after reading last week's devotions? (If you are participating as a group or family take time to discuss those desired changes.)

_____

_____

_____

_____

Think about a personal example in your life that demonstrates the truth of the devotions. (If you are participating as a group or family take time to share some of the stories with each other.)

_____

_____

_____

In their hearts humans plan their course,
but the Lord establishes their steps.
Proverbs 16:9 -

The Chief of Staff of Multi-National Corps-Iraq, a Brigadier General, commented that the only constant in war is change. Soldiers learn early on in their Army career to be flexible. A common joke is a play on words using the Marine Corps motto of Semper Fidelis (Always Faithful), and changing it to Semper Gumbi. Gumbi is an old cartoon character that was a flexible doll-type individual that was rubbery and could move and stretch in any direction. "Semper Gumbi" is the Soldier's way of saying, "I always have to be flexible because I know the plan or mission is most likely going to change."

The biggest example of being Semper Gumbi is our length of deployment. The tour of duty was originally planned for twelve months and is now extended to fifteen months, and some leaders in Washington are talking about eighteen months.

Such changes are frustrating and cause varying degrees of heartache. Personal and family plans have to be changed or canceled; stress increases at the front and back at home. One Soldier I talked to yesterday told me that with this extension he would miss his wedding anniversary for the fourth year out of the last five. Another Soldier I know has missed four of six birthdays for his daughter.

It is important to realize that God is still in charge. When we experience such cataclysmic changes and shifts in our plans or life dreams, we don't need to overreact or panic. God has a larger plan and can bring good from any change that appears bad. The mature woman or man of God understands the importance of striving to remain optimistic and trusting God in a constantly changing world.

Speak and act as those who are going to be judged
by the law that gives freedom.
James 2:12

Today I am writing from beside a large pool, and sitting under a big umbrella for a little shade. I'm seated on a white wooden-slotted chair, and my notebook is resting on a table made much the same way. When I feel the need, I'm quenching my thirst with a bottle of Gatorade that is also on the table, and the temperature is well above 110 degrees and climbing. If I ignore the distant gun fire and the regular passing of helicopters over my head this could almost be a vacation spot at a nice location in the United States. I have taken a group of Soldiers to the International Zone in downtown Baghdad to a place called Freedom Rest. It was part of an old officers-club for the Iraqi Republican Guard. Now it serves as a place of respite for our Soldiers. It is an oasis in the midst of a war-torn land where Soldiers can come and try to rest, relax, and renew for a few days - Freedom Rest.

The men and women here are taking a breather from the fight for freedom. It is not an easy fight. Too many young men and women have died or lost legs and arms. The question might be asked, "Is freedom worth fighting for?"

Senators John McCain and Lindsey Graham were recently here in Iraq on U.S. Independence Day. Senator McCain spoke to the over one hundred and sixty new citizens, and almost six hundred re-enlisting Soldiers. Senator McCain talked about the horror of war, the pain and the hurt, but then he said, "War is not the worst thing." He went on to talk about the freedom we celebrate every Fourth of July. He pointed out the worst thing is people who fail to understand or grasp that the lack of freedom can be more devastating than war.

Those who walk with Jesus know true freedom. God calls us who have that freedom to speak and act in accordance with the liberty we enjoy because of God's grace and love.

113

Men of Zebulun, experienced soldiers prepared for battle
with every type of weapon,
to help David with undivided loyalty...
1 Chronicles 12:33

As part of the time at Freedom Rest, we require each group to watch a movie and then participate in a discussion about the movie. We have brought numerous Soldiers to Freedom Rest for this program, using different chaplains as facilitators. We've shown various movies, "Facing the Giants," "The End of The Spear," and yesterday we viewed "The Chronicles of Narnia." The intent is to stimulate discussions that will help Soldiers contemplate and deal with issues and thoughts that are part of life in combat.

"The Chronicles of Narnia" movie is a wonderful tale that comes from the writings of C.S. Lewis about four children (two brothers and two sisters) who find their way to a mystical land that is in the grasp of the evil white witch. Yet, many of the inhabitants of Narnia know of and have faith and hope in Aslan. A long held belief is that Aslan, a lion, will bring peace and freedom when the two sons of Adam and two daughters of Eve come to the land.

The story that unfolds is one of betrayal, trust, temptation, loyalty, courage, desire, dishonesty, truthfulness, strength of family, and sacrifice. The youngest brother is pulled toward the evil side of things through the temptation and desire for power and pleasure. His weakness and betrayal leads to pain and sorrow. Through acts of great bravery, selfless service, and tremendous sacrifice, Aslan and the forces of good triumph over evil. Our Soldiers engage in powerful discussions concerning this analogy and how it applies to us today as we fight evil, feel forgotten, and are tempted to give up in the face of overwhelming circumstances.

Have you thought about the values in your life? You have been called by God to be a person of loyalty, to demonstrate the courage to do the right thing, and to be willing to give of yourself for others benefit! Make it your desire and mission to answer that call.

He has shown you, O mortal, what is good.
And what does the Lord require of you?
To act justly and to love mercy and to walk humbly with your God.
Micah 6:8

There is one final lesson based on the Fourth of July Naturalization and Re-enlistment ceremony that was conducted here. After the prayer, the swearing in as citizens, the oath of re-enlistment, the speeches, some music, and a video from the President of The United States; Senator Lindsey Graham led everyone in saying the Pledge of Allegiance. It was quite a sight, and an overwhelming feeling to be standing next to Senator McCain, surrounded by literally thousands of Soldiers, Sailors, Airmen, Marines, and Civilians all declaring together the words of our pledge. Yet, I wonder how many people comprehend and agree with the words. One part of the pledge has become especially controversial with some people and groups. This is how the pledge reads today, *"I pledge allegiance to the Flag of the United States of America, and to the Republic for which it stands, <u>one Nation under God</u>, indivisible, with liberty and justice for all."* The section underlined is the controversial part I'm referring to.

What does it mean to be a nation under God? Does such a declaration demand anything of that nation and people? I would say yes, it does. What would a God of justice, care, and compassion demand of that nation? More important and appropriate, what does God ask of you as a citizen of a nation that says we are "One Nation under God?" My personal answer is found in the "Micah Mandate." God lets us know in this verse from Micah that his expectation of us is to act justly, to love mercy, and to walk humbly with Him.

Do you consider yourself a person under God? If so adopt these calls from Micah as your personal mandates for how you live your life.

Be on your guard; stand firm in the faith; be courageous; be strong.
1 Corinthians 16:13

Yesterday I went on a special mission with a group of men from the Iraqi government. We flew in several Blackhawk helicopters from the International Zone in downtown Baghdad to Amerli. Amerli is a small town outside the larger city of Tuz, about 70 miles north of Baquba, the largest city in the Diyala province of Iraq. The people of this small town were barbarically attacked a few days ago by a large vehicle-borne improvised explosive device that literally vaporized one entire city block and destroyed another 2 to 3 blocks. Over 105 people were killed and another 250 were wounded. The explosion took place in the central-market area of Amerli, and many of those killed were women and children.

Three of the men who were with me were members of the Iraqi Parliament, and the senior member of the group was a Muslim Cleric. There were over a thousand people gathered near the blast site when we flew into Amerli. They were angry and still in shock, but they were also glad to see any help arrive. The team from Iraq distributed money to the community to help in the rebuilding effort. Then the cleric who was with us gave a speech at the blast site. It was quite a powerful moment with all the hurting people gathered around and the terrible destruction surrounding us. From the blast crater, we walked through the town to the local mosque, where another speech was given.

One of the points made by the cleric was that even wild animals don't kill masses of other animals. "These al-Qaeda thugs are worse than wild animals," he concluded.

God is calling us to be women and men of courage. Reach out beyond yourself, and stand strong against the "wild animals" you face in life.

Husbands, love your wives, just as Christ loved the church
and gave himself up for her.
Ephesians 5:25

A young chaplain I visited at a Forward Operating Base in southern Baghdad told me that he had missed three out of the last four of his wedding anniversaries. We were stationed together at another installation in the United States. I know his wife, and I'm sure she is very understanding, but it is still difficult and frustrating to miss such major events in a family's life.

Today, as I write this, it is my wedding anniversary, and obviously, I'm in Iraq and not back in the United States. I sent her some flowers through the internet (and she loved them), and I also sent numerous cards, but none of that compares with physically being present and conveying love in person.

Yet, in some ways our marriage has grown stronger over the years due in some measure to the separations we have endured because of deployments and Army exercises. Like most couples we have struggled with issues such as finances, communications, and marital/family expectations. Despite all of those things we have maintained our commitment to each other, and at times the unwanted separations helped us to realize how blessed we are to have each other and that has strengthened our love.

I would not recommend, nor do I desire such long times of being apart. However, as with most things, if you approach them with a positive attitude, even situations like being deployed to war and separated for 15 months can be used to foster growth and result in a positive outcome. Resolve to love your spouse and those closest to you despite any circumstance or situation. Determine in your heart and mind to grow and develop in the midst of life's challenges.

Therefore, I tell you, her many sins have been forgiven—
as her great love has shown.
But whoever has been forgiven little loves little.
Luke 7:47

The temperature was near 120 degrees; all of us were fully geared up with heavy body armor, helmets, and additional combat items. Those conditions would be enough to sap anyone's energy, but the young medic in front of me also had a large, heavy medical aide bag to carry. It was mid-afternoon, there was no shade, and we had been out in the sun for a couple hours in an area where high vigilance was required. I noticed this Soldier seemed to be bending over and "resting" a little more with each passing minute. I went up, placed my hand on his shoulder and told him what an inspiration he was. I let him know how much I valued his service and willingness to take the extra burden in order to care for wounded Soldiers. I offered him a drink from the bottle of water I had and then told him to hang in there in these tough conditions and what a great job he was doing. It was all he needed; that word of encouragement and act of kindness brought a tired smile to his face. He stood up little straighter under the heavy burden of his protective gear, hiked up his aide bag, and began to check on the welfare of others.

Jesus understood how a little encouragement could make a big difference in someone's life. The story that surrounds today's Bible verse demonstrates the principle when Jesus not only recognizes the kind acts of the woman involved, but also uses her service as a teaching opportunity.

A little support by way of a kind word or gesture can go a long way towards helping another person. Are you an encourager? Try offering a kind word to someone today; you'll be blessed and so will they.

Take a few minutes to review the devotions you read during this past week. Write down three key lessons you learned. What aspect of the week's devotions resonates most with you? (If you are participating as a group or family take time to discuss these key lessons.)

_____
_____
_____
_____

Were there any aspects of the devotions that you had trouble identifying with? (If you are participating as a group or family take time to discuss the troubling portions.)

_____
_____
_____
_____

Write down names of people you know who might be struggling with some of the points from the devotions. Take time to pray for each person. (If you are participating as a group, or family take time to pray for the people identified.)

_____
_____
_____
_____

What changes do you feel God is calling you to make after reading last week's devotions? (If you are participating as a group or family take time to discuss those desired changes.)

_____
_____
_____
_____

Think about a personal example in your life that demonstrates the truth of the devotions. (If you are participating as a group or family take time to share some of the stories with each other.)

_____
_____
_____
_____

But as for you, continue in what you have learned and have become
convinced of, because you know those from whom you learned it and
how from infancy you have known the Holy Scriptures, which are
able to make you wise
for salvation through faith in Christ Jesus.
2 Timothy 3:14-15

The Soldier providing medical aid to the wounded gunner of the
vehicle was still a teenager, yet he worked with a sense of calm control
and practiced skill. Another Soldier stood in front of a senior officer
who was visiting Iraq on a fact-finding mission and responded to the
officer with a sense of deep understanding and professionalism. As with
the first Soldier, this specialist was also still in her teens.

Observing our young Soldiers, I can't help but be impressed by
their commitment and dedication. Their performance is inspiring. As
I thought about these young men and women and my own children
back home, I pondered how much more difficult and complicated
life is today compared to when I was growing up. The influences and
temptations to give into undisguised sin are much greater today and
seem to be growing. Negative influences, old and new, challenge young
people on a continual basis to take the path of the convenient wrong
and not make the more difficult choice to take the wise, sometimes
more challenging correct path. I thank God for the young Soldiers
who have stood up, stepped up, and taken a higher path during these
changing and difficult times.

One thing has not changed. The best and highest way is still with
God. Paul's guidance in Timothy is good for us and our children.
We are always called to continue in the way of God. Be a person who
stands up and steps up to take a higher path during these shifting and
challenging times.

And walk in the way of love, just as Christ loved us
and gave himself up for us
as a fragrant offering and sacrifice to God.
Ephesians 5:2

I am on my way home for a two-week break. I am flying over the United States on an aircraft that is bringing a group of Soldiers back from Iraq for our mid-tour leave. I'm excited about being home for a little over two weeks, spending time with my family, attending a conference, and putting Iraq and the war behind me for a short time.

We flew out of an airfield in Baghdad. It took us a couple days to get out because of big dust storms, but early one morning I flew out of our area of operations. We marched out to the flight line toward a C-17 Globemaster that was sitting on the edge of the runway. There were about fifteen of us on this flight, a small number for such a big plane, and they had us load through the small front door usually used by the crew. Soldiers usually load the plane by going through the large rear entrance and up the cargo ramp.

But today we were not the primary mission of this flight. Inside the plane were seven neatly arranged coffins. Each one had a U.S. flag that was carefully draped over it. It was amazing how quiet it was as we crawled into our nylon-webbed seats. The Air Force crew was purposely and respectfully securing the coffins, and everyone felt a kinship as well as a sense of awe and reverence as we gazed at the stars and stripes of red, white, and blue and reflected on the men who lay underneath.

We landed at Kuwait International Airport where our brothers, six Army and one Marine, were offloaded. Everyone on board participated in a ceremony to honor the seven warriors who sacrificed their lives for a greater cause. I had the great privilege to offer a prayer for these brave warriors and their grieving families.

True freedom demands sacrifice. We are truly free because of Jesus' sacrifice, and we are blessed beyond measure! May we use that freedom and blessing to share the love of God with a hurting world.

So you also must be ready,
because the Son of Man will come at an hour
when you do not expect him.
Matthew 24:44

Fort Worth, where my conference was held, is a great city. There are some fantastic museums, Texas Christian University, good food, and Fort Worth still maintains a little bit of the old west at the Stockyards. My wife is with me and our hotel was in the old downtown Stockyard area. We decided to walk around the Stockyards and see the sites. At one point an old train locomotive steamed into the area, pulling some vintage passenger cars, that people could ride on for a small fee. A little later some cowboys in all their gear and on some big horses actually had a miniature cattle drive down the main street. The cowboys drove the big longhorn cattle mere feet from where we stood.

Then we walked to some shops and listened to a live country band playing on the sidewalk. At the same time a little farther down the way, a group of cowboys and cowgirls put on a short Wild West re-enactment. At some point during this show my wife and I had made it just past the edge of the crowd and were heading into one of the shops.

As with most of these shows there were some good guys and some bad guys. They were just at the point of the big confrontation as we stepped over the old bricks that lined the sidewalk and made our way into the shop. Of course, the confrontation included a gun fight, and all the players started firing their weapons at that moment.

I guess I was still in the combat mode, and not ready for gunfire while shopping in Fort Worth. So, much to the shock of my wife, I dove to the floor of the shop as the shots rang out. I quickly got up, and we laughed, but it made me think about God's call for us to always be ready. Too often we have accepted behaviors contrary to God's design as common place and okay, when they actually pose a threat to the collective human good. Be aware and ready.

Honor your father and your mother,
so that you may live long in the land the Lord your God is giving you.
Exodus 20:12

The task must not have been very easy. Now we laugh about it in our family, but the stories indicate the true nature of the situation. I was a "hand-full" growing up and especially as a young boy. Long before they were made of colorful nylon, had quick release straps, and retractable cords, my Mom made and used a harness for me. It was not a high-tech device that kept me from escaping but rather an old seat belt and some clothes-line cord sewed together and made to fit so tight I could not squirm away.

My Mom said it was all she could do to keep me from wandering away, especially with my brother and sister, two and three years younger, also in the mix. Mom said the homemade harness got her many disapproving looks from other moms and even some derogatory comments, but it was the only way to make sure I did not get lost.

That is typical of what I know my Mom and other mothers have to deal with as part of the challenge of raising children. Good parenting is fun and rewarding, but it is also hard work and demands sacrifice. It is right and fitting that we honor our parents, plus it is an expectation of God.

As part of my R & R time, I went home to Ohio to visit my Dad and my Mom (who is struggling with a debilitating illness). The visit was unplanned, but it was so good to see my parents and in a small way try to honor them. Some of you have been hurt by your parents, but I encourage you to try to honor them or maybe just take those first steps toward forgiveness. Forgiveness does not mean you condone past hurtful actions, but it is the beginning of true healing and liberty for you, and perhaps others as well.

Day after day, in the temple courts and from house to house, they never stopped teaching and proclaiming the good news that Jesus is the Messiah.
Acts 5:42

The United States Military is engaged in a great and noble task in Afghanistan and Iraq. Sadly, as of yet, it has not progressed as many folks had hoped it would. The best intentions have resulted in many deaths and not the progress or restoration of justice that was expected. Still the Soldiers who are engaged every day around the world are working hard on behalf of the United States to do good things. I don't know if they would echo this quote by Helen Keller, but I thought it was interesting and applicable: *"I long to accomplish a great and noble task, but it is my chief duty to accomplish humble tasks as though they were great and noble. The world is moved along not only by the mighty shoves of its heroes but also by the aggregate of the tiny pushes of each honest worker."*

Helen Keller's quote sums up in many ways what being a Soldier and Soldiering is all about. Most of the men and women serving in the Army know that they are part of a great team effort. They each have small, simple, humble tasks to perform that contribute to the whole of a great and noble purpose. Our leaders are fantastic people and often their heroic shoves "move the world," but primarily it is the totality of the many Soldiers "tiny pushes" that cause the Army and our nation to find success.

As servants of God, we are people who should relate to this quote. It is good to have far-reaching goals that are great and noble. God needs such leaders and heroes of the faith who strive for great and noble purposes, but God also wants us to accomplish those every day, humble tasks and to be part of the Kingdom of God that touches others with millions of tiny pushes. Just as the early church had those who worked day after day to bring good news to others, so too, should we work to daily help the cause of sharing God's love.

...But as for me and my household, we will serve the Lord.
Joshua 24:15

One of the best known persons to have been a victim of the Nazi regime during WWII was Victor E. Frankl. He wrote this, *"We who lived in concentration camps can remember the men who walked through the huts comforting others, giving away their last piece of bread. They may have been few in number, but they offer sufficient proof that everything can be taken from a man but one thing: the last of his freedoms – to choose one's attitude in any given set of circumstances, to choose one's own way."*

At an event I attended while at Fort Hood, I spoke with two different spouses. Their situations are very similar. They were raised in a healthy environment; they both are intelligent and hold good jobs. Both spouses have two children and are married to men who are good, reliable husbands. Obviously, there are aspects about these two and their families that I don't know about, but for the most part their basic circumstances are the same. Yet, one of them sees almost everything in a negative light. She feels as if she is "owed" because of the sacrifice of her husband's service in the Army and especially his combat deployments to Iraq and Afghanistan. The other woman has almost a continual positive outlook and strives to reach out to as many people as she can and share what she considers all her blessings. Her husband has also had numerous deployments to combat, and they have spent many months separated. Her response is to gratefully serve God.

How are you choosing to live with what is going on in your life? You can honor God by continuing to serve Him honorably, regardless of circumstances. Choose today to try to see the positive side of circumstances or if it just seems to all be bad, choose to learn and grow from these times.

Don't let anyone look down on you because you are young, but set an example for the believers in speech, in life, in love, in faith and in purity.
1 Timothy 4:12

A sergeant was seated next to me on the plane as we flew back to Iraq. During our flight we started talking, and at some point in the conversation, he asked me what was the toughest thing chaplains had to do in combat. As we talked that out, we both agreed about the hardship of death and everything that is associated with fellow Soldiers being killed in action. The sergeant related to me the hurt and sorrow he had experienced in the loss of a number of his fellow warriors. He said he did not know how the chaplains could work in that realm on a regular basis, saying it would emotionally wear him out. He told me he had been especially impacted by the death of one particular friend of his.

The friend was killed by a sniper after their convoy had been hit by an IED. He talked about what a wonderful and moving memorial ceremony had been conducted for this Soldier. The Soldier that was killed in action had been a strong, committed Christian, and he had lived as an example of Christ's influence in his life. The sergeant said that after the death he reflected on the life of his friend, and it inspired him to try and live a more faithful life. The influence of that Soldier's life had a significant impact and is what the verse from 1 Timothy is all about.

I want to encourage you to take a look at your life in light of this concept. Would others you work and live with want to be like you because of the influence God has made in your life? Are you an example to others in word, conduct, love, spirit, faith, and purity? That should be our goal.

Take a few minutes to review the devotions you read during this past week. Write down three key lessons you learned. What aspect of the week's devotions resonates most with you? (If you are participating as a group or family take time to discuss these key lessons.)

_____

_____

_____

_____

Were there any aspects of the devotions that you had trouble identifying with? (If you are participating as a group or family take time to discuss the troubling portions.)

_____

_____

_____

_____

Write down names of people you know who might be struggling with some of the points from the devotions. Take time to pray for each person. (If you are participating as a group, or family take time to pray for the people identified.)

_____

_____

_____

_____

What changes do you feel God is calling you to make after reading last week's devotions? (If you are participating as a group or family take time to discuss those desired changes.)

_____

_____

_____

_____

Think about a personal example in your life that demonstrates the truth of the devotions. (If you are participating as a group or family take time to share some of the stories with each other.)

_____

_____

_____

_____

Then the church throughout Judea, Galilee and Samaria enjoyed a
time of peace and was strengthened. Living in the fear of the Lord
and encouraged by the Holy Spirit, it increased in numbers.
Acts 9:31

My leave (Army word for vacation) time is behind me now, and I
must begin to re-focus on the mission ahead. A number of my friends
and fellow Soldiers here have expressed their gladness to see me. The
comments most often sound something like, "Welcome back," or "Glad
you are back." I suppose a common response to those comments might
be, "It is good to be back." However, it was hard to leave my wife and
family again. To say I was glad to be back would not be 100% true. I
try not to dwell on the fact that due to our extension, I still have over six
months before I can go back home. Yet, I can honestly say that in some
ways I am glad to be back, because I feel as if I have a responsibility,
and I don't want to shirk my duty to provide ministry to our Soldiers.

Wherever we are God wants to use us. Sometimes our greatest
witness for God, and our ability to show Godly love and care to others
who are hurting, is found in the times we face difficult and even painful
circumstances. It would be very easy to get down about something that
was behind us, or to be fearful, angry, or depressed about what might be
ahead. But that process is not helpful, nor is it what God expects of us.

Ralph Waldo Emerson said, *"What lies behind us and what lies before
us are tiny matters compared to what lies within us."* This is especially
true of those who have accepted Jesus into their lives, and can look at
what is truly important. We have the Holy Spirit, God actually living
within us, encouraging us, guiding us, bringing us peace and wiping
fear away. Take heart and rejoice because of the presence of God in your
life. Allow that presence to guide you to an attitude and life that exalts
God and encourages those around you.

Therefore, as God's chosen people, holy and dearly loved,
clothe yourselves with compassion, kindness,
humility, gentleness and patience.
Colossians 3:12

A report indicated that suicide rates in the Army were up to historical levels. The chaplains, mental-health providers, and others are trying to develop and implement ways to lower the number of suicides among Soldiers and other military members.

A friend sent me this story. Tim was walking home from school when the boy ahead of him stumbled and fell. The load he was carrying scattered over the ground. Tim stopped and helped pick up the boy's backpack, some gym clothes, a jacket, and a bag of other items. The boy's name turned out to be Curtis, and Tim offered to help him carry his stuff the rest of the way home. While walking, they found out they both liked football and video games.

Tim's home was on the way, and the two boys stopped and had a snack, and played some video games. Both boys enjoyed the afternoon, and then Tim helped Curtis home. Throughout the rest of their school life, the two were not best buddies, but they did remain friends and kept in contact. As their senior year came near and graduation time was around the corner, Curtis ran into Tim at the mall and asked if he could buy him a soda. As they sat and talked, Curtis brought up the day they had met. "Did you ever wonder why I had so much stuff with me that day?" asked Curtis. "I had cleaned out all my things, and was planning to go home and kill myself. Your kindness and that afternoon of friendship caused me to stop and re-look my plans. Your helping me that day saved my life."

God calls us to be men and women of kindness who help those in need. You may not know if your efforts have a significant impact, but it will make a difference. More importantly, it is the right and Godly thing to do. Show some unexpected kindness today.

Woe to you who are complacent in Zion, and to you who feel secure on Mount Samaria, you notable men of the foremost nation, to whom the people of Israel come!
Amos 6:1

Be alert and of sober mind. Your enemy the devil prowls around like a roaring lion looking for someone to devour.
1 Peter 5:8

While walking back to the office with one of my Soldiers, the siren indicating possible incoming rockets or mortars suddenly began to wail, warning of an impending attack. At this point incoming fire is cause for concern, but the reaction is not so immediately concerning; rather it is more "wait and see." So we got a little chuckle as we saw some newly arrived Soldiers dive to the ground, then get up and run at a frantic pace to a nearby building. No rounds impacted in our area, but the truth is those new Soldiers did the right thing.

Recently, a young woman was killed when shrapnel from a rocket attack hit her in the head. Her friends were upset because they knew if she had just gotten down on the ground when the warning sounded, she would not have been killed.

Today, I was heading to an early morning meeting when I heard the whine of incoming rockets. Five rounds impacted in the area. The first two rockets were not too close, and I along with other Soldiers walking at that point simply paused, crouched down a little, and then started off again. The next three rockets were much closer, impacting near enough to knock us down. After that we jumped up and ran for the nearest bunker.

Too often we treat sin and temptation in our life like those rockets. We forget how "deadly" it can be and don't take immediate and appropriate action until sometimes it is too late. Don't become complacent in your spiritual life, especially in those actions that keep you protected from sin.

And the God of all grace, who called you to his eternal glory in Christ, after you have suffered a little while, will himself restore you and make you strong, firm and steadfast.
1 Peter 5:10

How do we gain spiritual strength and grow in our lives? How do we work toward being better women and men? A large part of it comes from the way God has established us. The freedom God has given to us means that we face the joys and sufferings of life. The fact that God allows us to undergo the hard times and suffering is significant. It is often the fires of suffering that produce the greatest growth in our spiritual life. It is interesting to listen to some of the stories from Soldiers in Afghanistan and Iraq. The difficulties and trials they have endured while in combat and on the home front are not something they would like to go through again. However, most of them recognize how those times and situations have made them better.

I remember a time when I was stationed with the 82nd Airborne Division at Fort Bragg, North Carolina. One weekend my wife and I were out in the region that is known for the pottery that is made by the locals. At one shop where we stopped, the pottery was made right there, and the owner was proudly showing us some aspects of the operation. Some of the pottery had colors that were obviously more brilliant than others. When I asked about the colors, I was told it was mostly a matter of how the piece was fired and how many times.

It is often the same with us in our lives. We think that we are a good work, but then we are thrust into a fiery furnace of hardship and trial. Amazingly, if we trust in God and persevere, we often come out as an even stronger and better person. If you are under a painful trial, or enduring a series of setbacks, hang in there and know that you can emerge better for it.

But while everyone was sleeping,
his enemy came and sowed weeds among the wheat, and went away.
Matthew 13:25

There is a battle going on, and it is dangerous. As I write this, it appears that the number of Soldiers killed and wounded is finally starting to go down in frequency. That is great news, but sadly we still have Soldiers who are killed on a regular basis. One of the difficulties in this combat zone is identifying the enemy. Those who are intent on killing our Soldiers or killing and bringing violence to the civilian population, basically look and dress the same as the population we are trying to protect. Many people carry weapons, which makes the task of identifying bad guys even more problematic. The most difficult enemy to identify is the bomber who hides the bomb and tries to fit in with the rest of the population.

One attack was carried out by a younger man who seemed to simply ride his bike toward a group of U.S. Soldiers who were out on patrol with a group of Iraqi Security Forces. It appears that some of the Iraqi Soldiers may have known the bicyclist but did not immediately recognize or discern any danger. At one point they did direct him to stop his approach toward the group, but he continued on and then detonated a bomb he had strapped to his body. One U.S. Soldier was killed and two Iraqi Soldiers were killed. Following the event, one of the Soldiers said, "I saw the enemy but did not recognize him as a danger."

As Christians we must understand that we too are in a battle and that we face an enemy that wants to destroy us. One of our tasks is to identify the enemy, who at times may seem harmless, but is not. Once identified, we must take a stand against that enemy. Verse 13 of Ephesians 6 says, "When the day of evil comes." It does not say "if" it comes. We will face enemy attempts to hurt us. Are you ready? Don't be caught sleeping.

Just as a body, though one, has many parts,
but all its many parts form one body, so it is with Christ.
1 Corinthians 12:12

The Command Sergeant Major of the Multi-National Corps-Iraq was standing with me on the roof of our Command Headquarters. He had just returned from a long trip up north to the Mosul area. We were there to discuss some other issues, but we paused to talk about his trip. I was interested in how it had gone and how he was doing personally. During the course of our conversation, he told me of one incident that caused me to pause and think.

As the Command Sergeant Major (CSM) and his security detail were driving down their route, they noticed something that did not look right about the road. After the CSM and the chief of the security team conferred on their radios, they decided to pass by on the far side of the road. As the second vehicle in their convoy passed by the questionable area, an IED exploded in the middle of the road, and the convoy began to take small arms fire. Since the vehicle was off to the side and not over the IED the explosion only caused minor damage. The gunners on the Humvees immediately opened fire, and the drivers quickly got out of the line of enemy fire. They then maneuvered to allow our Soldiers to better engage the enemy. Others in the group were quickly radioing information to each other and to the higher headquarters.

Each person caught in that attack (the radio operators, the gunners, the medics, and the spotters) played a key and vital role, in the decision of where and how to proceed. That principle is true in the family of God. Every person plays a key and vital role in whatever way they serve God. You need to understand that what you do in your service to God is important. Keep it up.

Whoever walks in integrity walks securely,
but whoever takes crooked paths will be found out.
Proverbs 10:9

One of the more meaningful and moving moments that happens in the nightly Battle Update Assessment at MNC-I Headquarters is the Hero Tribute. The tribute is presented twice a week by one of the chaplains who work for me on the MNC-I staff. During that time every person in the Joint Operation Center stands to their feet while a tribute is read, and a slide commemorating one of our Soldiers, Sailors, Airmen, or Marines who has been killed in action is displayed on our big screens. The chaplain who puts the tributes together does a great job of creating a good picture in words of each of these men and women. It is amazing to listen and hear about some of these remarkable young warriors.

One recent account really caught my attention as the chaplain read some of the quotes made by people who knew this particular Soldier back home. The quotes described a young man who had always been a faithful follower of Jesus. He was involved in numerous activities and organizations back home, and he had made a positive impression on what seemed like his entire hometown. What really struck me was a word that came up in two of the quotes from those who best knew this amazing young man who died serving his country. That word was *integrity*.

The young man's pastor from his hometown and his old boss spoke of his integrity, and how they could depend on him to do the right thing. That commitment to always do the right thing is the kind of integrity that David was referring to in today's Scripture reading. We are called to be people of integrity. You can start that process by committing yourself to do the right thing.

Take a few minutes to review the devotions you read during this past week. Write down three key lessons you learned. What aspect of the week's devotions resonates most with you? (If you are participating as a group or family take time to discuss these key lessons.)

_____

_____

_____

_____

Were there any aspects of the devotions that you had trouble identifying with? (If you are participating as a group or family take time to discuss the troubling portions.)

_____

_____

_____

_____

Write down names of people you know who might be struggling with some of the points from the devotions. Take time to pray for each person. (If you are participating as a group, or family take time to pray for the people identified.)

_____

_____

_____

_____

What changes do you feel God is calling you to make after reading last week's devotions? (If you are participating as a group or family take time to discuss those desired changes.)

_____

_____

_____

_____

Think about a personal example in your life that demonstrates the truth of the devotions. (If you are participating as a group or family take time to share some of the stories with each other.)

So you also must be ready,
because the Son of Man will come
at an hour when you do not expect him.
Matthew 24:44

Yesterday our command conducted a special ceremony to remember the events of September 11, 2001. The ceremony was reflective, honoring, uplifting, and memorable. The event was conducted late in the morning, but only a few hours later, that positive atmosphere was turned upside down when an extremely large rocket landed in the midst of a heavily populated area of our camp. This rocket carried an explosive payload about two to three times the norm.

The damage that was done was extensive. A number of vehicles were destroyed, buildings were damaged, a large crater opened in the roadway, and other property was blown up and rendered useless. The chapel where we hold our services, and where members of my team work, was hit. Shrapnel from the explosion shattered windows, damaged the entrance door, put holes in the roof, and knocked down several items.

All this was upsetting and costly, but the worst and most costly consequence of the attack was eleven people were wounded and one person was killed.

I was in the area close to the impact, and was the first chaplain to arrive at our medical clinic. I was told that one person was not going to live. As I walked into the treatment area, there were patients on all the tables and a lot of blood. Then someone told me that a Soldier I knew well was at the end of the room. I was worried he might be the one expected to die. He was badly wounded but would live. The young man who was mortally wounded was in another part of the clinic. I got there and held his hand just as he died, so I prayed for him right as the doctor pronounced him dead.

Once again we are reminded to stay vigilant and alert. We must be ready, for life is fleeting and often short. Readiness in this instance has several aspects, but most importantly means knowing Jesus.

Let us not become weary in doing good,
for at the proper time we will reap a harvest if we do not give up.
Galatians 6:9

The Deputy MNC-I chaplain, a wonderful man of God named Dave Waters, was talking to me about the number of Christian men who go through twenty, thirty, forty years or more serving the Lord only to falter at a later point in life. The concept he used was a take-off on Paul's theme of running a race, and he said too many did not finish well.

I think there are numerous reasons why some folks fade or falter later in their life. Nobody begins the race with the goal of not finishing well. The concept for most folks is that they will actually grow and develop over the years, and finish strong.

One of the things we see with our Soldiers as they get toward the end of their twelve or fifteen months of deployment is that they get tired and weary, and that often results in bad decision making. A recent mental-health assessment done by our medical command showed a correlation between length of tours and Soldier problems, including mistreatment or even abuse of enemy fighters. Part of that equation is that Soldiers get weary and lose focus to the point of not taking what they know is the right course of action. There are some measures that can be put into place to help Soldiers offset the tendency to become overly weary. There is a need to make sure they get the proper rest, care for injuries, eat nutritious food, and obtain needed training and education.

As Christians we too run the risk of allowing ourselves to get weary and tired. That weariness can cause us to get off course and lose our spiritual focus. We can help prevent that type of breakdown by resting in the Lord, seeking and providing care when folks are hurt, spending time in worship, and seeking the needed training and education of God's Word and other Godly principles.

Do your best to present yourself to God as one approved, a worker who does not need to be ashamed and who correctly handles the word of truth.
2 Timothy 2:15

He was a true hero. During an ambush, the convoy he was a part of was attacked with an improvised explosive device. The convoy was then assaulted with a barrage of small arms fire. The Soldier's actions during that engagement saved the lives of other Soldiers. The vehicle he was in was hit by the bomb explosion, causing it to flip over. Soon a fire was burning in the vehicle. He was able to quickly free himself, but went back to help his fellow Soldiers in the vehicle. As he was assisting these Soldiers, the enemy opened fire from a nearby building. This courageous Soldier quickly spotted the point where the hostile fire was coming from and engaged the enemy. His action effectively caused the dangerous weapons fire on his fellow Soldiers to be lifted from them and directed his way.

Later, when the Soldier was being recognized for his actions in combat, he said he was only trying to do his best. He said his constant prayer is, "Lord, give me the courage and strength to do my best."

J.R.R. Tolkien once said, *"It is not the strength of the body that counts, but the strength of the spirit."* Too often we mistakenly believe that great acts are the dominion of the strong bodied men and women, but great acts are more often found by those who possess a strong heart and a simple desire to do their best.

Each day our goal as Christians should simply be to do our best. We must strive to be loving and kind, to not let color, appearance, or belief keep us from pursuing the Godly goal of demonstrating love and kindness to others. We are called to do our best as servants of God who unashamedly grasp and appropriately apply the truth of God in our daily lives.

If you really keep the royal law found in Scripture,
"Love your neighbor as yourself," you are doing right.
James 2:8

A Sailor I know told me she felt she had not been treated with dignity and respect in her office. I could tell she was feeling very low. As it turned out, she had been implicated in some questionable actions. It appeared that at least some of her perception was due to her getting in trouble, and the repercussions of that trouble. However, I agreed with her that there is never a good reason to not treat someone with dignity and respect.

Major General (MG) Melvin Zais said, *"You cannot expect a Soldier to be proud if you humiliate him. You cannot expect a Soldier to be brave if you abuse and cower him. You cannot expect a Soldier to be strong if you break him. You cannot ask for respect and obedience and willingness to assault hot LZs, hump back-breaking ridges, destroy dug-in emplacements if your Soldier has not been treated with the respect and dignity which fosters unit esprit and personal pride."*

The words of MG Zais apply to people in all walks of life. Everyone deserves to be treated in a way that upholds her or his dignity. Sometimes we Christians are not very good with this concept of treating everyone with dignity and respect. We treat those we agree with and who are "Christians in good standing" just fine. But sometimes those who are opposed to us or those who have sin we recognize are treated with disdain or even cruelty. One church in Kansas went so far as to demonstrate and yell at the funerals of Soldiers to protest the Army's homosexual policy. Whether or not their view is wrong or right is secondary to their unwarranted and un-Godly acts of cruelty that stand contrary to God's expectations.

Christians should be the standard bearers for treating people with dignity and respect. Where do you stand? Make sure you are honoring others and treating them in a manner that demonstrates a love of neighbor.

Be on your guard;
stand firm in the faith; be courageous; be strong. Do everything in love.
1 Corinthians 16:13-14

"The key is not backing down." These words were what one senior Soldier described as a primary factor in creating the success of our forces driving down the violence and number of attacks in Iraq.

Yesterday the devotion ended with the question, "Where do you stand?" The question was asked in the context of treating other people we encounter with dignity and respect. The point and the mandate of God are clear. Christians should always treat others with respect and dignity. Yet, my experience and history teaches that we often miss that mark, and at times think we are justified in not treating others well because of their beliefs. Often there is a thought or concept that showing a person, even an enemy, dignity and respect is a sign of weakness. The other concept that concerns people is that they feel their actions of dignity and respect might be interrupted as approval of the other person's behavior. This is a legitimate concern, but not a concern that legitimizes improper action.

Treating others with dignity and respect may be interpreted wrong. Small minded and insecure persons may see such action as weak, but it is neither an indication of approval or of weakness. Jesus was the master of showing love and kindness, and conveying dignity and respect to all those He encountered. Yet, very few people would categorize Jesus as weak or approving of sinful behavior. There was no doubt that Jesus stood firm, and he wants to see the same in us.

We often laud the courage and strength it takes to stand up against wrong actions, and certainly that is a true value. But at times the real courage and strength comes in affirming the dignity of those we are opposed to, and treating them in an appropriate manner while still upholding our Christian values.

But God chose the foolish things of the world to shame the wise;
God chose the weak things of the world to shame the strong.
1 Corinthians 1:27

What does a real hero look like? I read the first-hand account of another of our amazing Soldiers who had died in battle by taking actions that saved the lives of his teammates. Perhaps the most remarkable aspect is he took an action that he probably knew would kill him. A grenade was tossed in an enclosed area where several Soldiers were located. By all accounts the Soldier who died could have gotten away from the immediate blast area, and in fact initially started to move that direction. He must have realized that his fellow Soldiers were not aware of where the grenade was. He turned and jumped on the grenade, saving his friends, but losing his own life.

I developed a picture in my own mind of what this Soldier hero looked like. I envisioned the perfect Soldier; you know a "Captain America" type guy, strong, powerful, eagle eyed, probably a nice set of airborne wings on his chest. So when I saw his picture, it surprised me a little bit to see a young, skinny guy with glasses, and even a few spots of acne. He might not have looked like the idea of a perfect Soldier, but he sure was a great one and a true hero.

I realized, as I thought about it, that we often do the same thing with how we think the perfect Christian should look or act. A picture of someone who is "good-looking," well-spoken, knowledgeable, and has enough money to meet all needs is what too many of us think. Not only are our thoughts shallow, but the truth is, God often uses just the opposite type of Christians to spread His Good News and to do great things. God takes what we often see as weak or flawed individuals, and uses them to accomplish wonderful and amazing things. God will use you the same way if you let Him.

Hatred stirs up conflict, but love covers over all wrongs.
Proverbs 10:12

What does it mean to be a combat chaplain? No single example would give a complete picture. A chaplain friend of mine reported an Easter Sunday story that could only happen in combat and is definitely foreign to pastors and believers in the United States. During the middle of his sermon, mortar fire interrupted the service. The rounds hit very close, knocking a few Soldiers down, and causing them to seek shelter. After a few minutes, everyone gathered back around the chaplain and continued the Easter Service.

Another chaplain expressed part of his ministry as one of presence. This is a common theme for all chaplains, being with their Soldiers and bringing God to the Soldiers and the Soldiers to God. The chaplains don't carry weapons. So, when the chaplains are out walking on patrol with their Soldiers, or riding in a convoy, or visiting a combat outpost totally unarmed in enemy territory, it is a significant statement of God's love for the Soldiers demonstrated through the presence of these committed chaplains. Some of our chaplains have walked hundreds of miles with their Soldiers and been on 40, 50, 60 patrols. As one chaplain put it, "The bonds developed when you get shot at, mortared, or bombed together go very deep."

Dave Curlin, an Infantry Battalion Chaplain and friend I visited at a remote Forward Operating Base, stated it best. He said, "I've decided the best thing I can do is try to love these very broken men with the love of Christ. I've learned to look past the cussing, swearing, off-color jokes, and anger. Instead I want to focus on the hurt and pain most of these Soldiers carry."

What these chaplains offer to the Soldiers is no different than what those people around you need; the active expression of God's love and care through your actions and listening ear. Show someone you care.

Take a few minutes to review the devotions you read during this past week. Write down three key lessons you learned. What aspect of the week's devotions resonates most with you? (If you are participating as a group or family take time to discuss these key lessons.)

_____

_____

_____

_____

Were there any aspects of the devotions that you had trouble identifying with? (If you are participating as a group or family take time to discuss the troubling portions.)

_____

_____

_____

_____

Write down names of people you know who might be struggling with some of the points from the devotions. Take time to pray for each person. (If you are participating as a group, or family take time to pray for the people identified.)

_____

_____

_____

_____

What changes do you feel God is calling you to make after reading last week's devotions? (If you are participating as a group or family take time to discuss those desired changes.)

_____

_____

_____

_____

Think about a personal example in your life that demonstrates the truth of the devotions. (If you are participating as a group or family take time to share some of the stories with each other.)

_____

_____

_____

_____

A gentle answer turns away wrath, but a harsh word stirs up anger....
but whoever heeds correction shows prudence.
Proverbs 15:1 and 5b

Today we search for wisdom from Proverbs. I was recently flying over Baghdad to attend a Memorial Ceremony for a Soldier who had been Killed in Action. After the ceremony I linked up with the Brigade Commander and flew to his Forward Operating Base (FOB) to meet with a couple chaplains who were having troubles. The one chaplain's issue had risen to a level where it was a combat distraction for the unit, and I needed to get involved.

The problems at this FOB with the involved chaplains were not simple, but much of the discord was due to not heeding the guidance found in the Proverbs. The younger chaplain felt as if he was being prevented from fully expressing his faith. Yet, when I looked into the matter, I found he had created animosity with almost everyone who had to work with him, peers and superiors alike. One of the primary concerns communicated by others was his unwillingness to make reasonable adjustments and accommodations.

I agreed with this younger chaplain that at least one of his superiors was wrong in the use of profanity and cursing. I also let him know that the expectations of his superiors were also legitimate, and he needed to strive to meet those expectations.

A good lesson for us is the guidance found above in verse one of Proverbs fifteen. If we need to correct someone, we need to do it prudently and gently. However, just as importantly is what the young chaplain failed to understand. We need to listen and heed correction, take it to heart, and make appropriate changes. That young chaplain's attitude actually hurt and deterred the cause of Christ, the exact opposite goal he had for his ministry. Don't fall in a similar trap. Listen to those around you, weigh their advice, and be willing to make changes when they are called for.

You, my brothers and sisters, were called to be free. But do not use your freedom to indulge the flesh; rather, serve one another humbly in love.
Galatians 5:13

The year was 1978, and I was a young platoon leader in Germany. The Army, as an organization, was still trying to get back on its feet after the great cultural changes of the sixties, the Vietnam War, and the subsequent draw down. One of the big issues was racial bias and discrimination. I can remember fights between black and white Soldiers, and abuse of minority Soldiers was not unusual.

The following humorous story, from an unknown source, is a good illustration of how at times we can be self-defeating in terms of living out our Christian faith when it comes to treating others who are different with kindness and love.

Many years ago Risa Silverman decided to take a long desired trip from Cleveland to Florida. She made the long drive to Miami, stopping at numerous hotels. However, in Miami she stopped at a hotel that did not accept Jews, so when she introduced herself as Mrs. Silverman, the clerk said, "I'm sorry, but we don't have any rooms available." Just then a guest came up and checked out. Mrs. Silverman was pleased and said, "Now there is a room available."

"I'm sorry." Replied the clerk. "Our hotel does not allow Jews." Mrs. Silverman said, "Jewish, I'm not Jewish; I'm Baptist." "Is that so," said the clerk. "If that is the case, you can tell me who the son of God is and where He was born." She answered, "Jesus and He was born in a stable."

"Okay, but why was He born in a stable?" the clerk retorted. Mrs. Silverman shot back, "Because a schmuck like you wouldn't let a Jew have a room."

The story is funny, but only if it doesn't really happen. Sadly, discrimination based on race, culture, and religion is still happening. Don't allow yourself to treat others badly because they are different. God calls us to be a people of love and kindness.

Then Jesus' disciples said, "Now you are speaking clearly
and without figures of speech."
John 16: 29

As our Soldiers prepare for different missions, they go over the plan
to accomplish the mission numerous times. The assigned tasks can be
varied, from moving spare parts by truck from Kuwait to Baghdad,
doing road clearance and looking for explosive devices, transporting
people through dangerous areas, conducting a raid to capture a known
terrorist leader, or responding to an enemy attack. One constant in
all missions is the attempt to make sure everyone participating in the
operation understands the purpose of the mission and how it is going
to be conducted. In order to meet that goal, the plans are presented,
as much as possible, to the Soldiers with an old adage in mind. We try
to use the principle of KISS, which stands for, *Keep It Simple Stupid.*

Sometimes we defeat our own efforts for trying to explain or share
the Good News of Jesus with others by being too complicated. As an
ordained minister, I can say that too often clergy are especially guilty
of this, using words and phrases that are hard to understand and don't
mean much to the person or persons being addressed. The concept
of simplicity may not be too impressive, but it is usually effective.
Certainly there are times when the principle of KISS might not apply,
but normally it is a good bet.

In the Scripture reading for today from the book of John, Jesus
communicated in a way that was simple and clear. Not only did the
people who heard Jesus understand Him, but His plain speaking also
led them to believe He came from God.

Today, as you strive to live a life that is pleasing to God, remember
to KISS. Simply show love and kindness to those around you and strive
to be obedient to God in all that you do. It is that simple.

But he said to me, "My grace is sufficient for you,
for my power is made perfect in weakness."
Therefore I will boast all the more gladly about my weaknesses,
so that Christ's power may rest on me.
2 Corinthians 12:9

The war that is being fought in Afghanistan and Iraq has brought some positive changes from previous wars and conflicts. The improvement in body armor is one of the biggest positive changes. Although it is still heavy, and at times cumbersome, the current armor has saved the life of many of our Soldiers. Nevertheless, it is lighter and more effective than past versions.

However, many of our troops that survive catastrophic attacks end up with grievous injuries. Where once a Soldier would have died in an attack he now lives. The armor protects his vital organs and his life, but he often loses legs and arms.

One young man who was in a Humvee that was hit by a roadside bomb had one of his legs severed just above his knee. He was evacuated through Germany and back to the United States. Once he was stable he began the long road to recovery. At one point the Soldier was speaking about his experience, and he said that once the shock was past, he realized that he needed to seek the direction of God for his future without one of his legs. He did not dwell on why he lost a leg, but instead he focused on what God now wanted or expected from him.

It is normal to question God or be angry when horrible things happen in our lives, but it is important not to dwell on the why. Without looking to God's desire for us in our "new" life, we run the risk of missing or delaying the awesome power and grace of God. Asking the question, "What do you want from me now Lord?" moves us forward instead of looking back. Despite our weaknesses God wants to use us in powerful ways that speak to His glory and power.

I long to dwell in your tent forever and
take refuge in the shelter of your wings.
Psalm 61:4

Whoever dwells in the shelter of the Most High will rest in the
shadow of the Almighty.
Psalm 91:1

The sun was not quite up, but the sky to the east was beginning to lighten, and the prospect of a brilliant sunrise lay ahead of me. I was running down one of the roads on Victory Base and simply enjoying the start of a new day. However, I was soon focused on something else. In recent days our camp has taken a lot of rocket fire. Two days ago seventeen rockets were fired at our camp and the result was three Soldiers killed in action and thirty-seven Soldiers wounded in action. This morning three explosions rocked our camp as I was out running. Not long after that, three more rockets came screaming into the camp and again brought destruction our way.

Several days ago, at a Forward Operating Base (FOB) just outside of Baghdad, a similar attack occurred. We have an "alarm" system that sometimes warns us of incoming fire from mortars and rockets. It is dependent on our radars acquiring the incoming rounds. The response of our Soldiers is to take shelter in one of the concrete bunkers scattered around base or to get down on the ground if no shelter is readily available. However, Soldiers are often slow to react or have grown lax in their response. One Soldier in the attack at the FOB did not get down and in the second blast was struck by shrapnel and killed.

There are times when all of us need to take shelter. Sometimes we need a physical shelter, and sometimes we need a spiritual shelter. God gives us a place to take a safe break and find shelter in God's peaceful presence that goes beyond our understanding. If you feel like you are under attack, try turning to God and asking for that peace.

Finally, all of you, be like-minded, be sympathetic,
love one another, be compassionate and humble.
1 Peter 3:8

Today I am in the country of Bahrain for a Conference hosted by the United States Central Command. We are primarily talking about religious-leader engagement by chaplains with the local clerics in the areas where they are assigned in Iraq or Afghanistan. Last night I went with some other chaplains to some markets so that I could buy my wife a gift for Christmas. I think I know what she will like; in fact, I'm sure that the unique jewelry I bought will be something she'll wear with joy and pride. However, some men don't always have good experiences as the following story from an unknown author illustrates.

A man asked his wife, "If you could have anything in the world for one day, what would you want?" "I'd love to be six again," he heard her reply. On the morning of her birthday, he got her up bright and early and off they went to a local theme park. What a day! He put her on every ride in the park: the Death Slide, the Screaming Loop roller coaster, the Wall of Fear, everything there was.

Amazing! Seven hours later she staggered out of theme park, her head reeling and her stomach upside down. Then they went to a McDonald's, where her husband ordered her a Big Mac, fries, and a cold chocolate shake. From there it was off to a movie, the latest Hollywood blockbuster, with popcorn, soft drink, and candy. It was a great, marvelous adventure.

Finally, they wobbled home and collapsed in bed. He leaned over and lovingly asked, "Well honey, what was it like being six again?" She opened one eye and moaned, "I meant my dress size." The moral of this story is the following: If a woman speaks and a man actually listens, he will still get it wrong. Okay, that is not always the case.

It is important that we listen to our spouses and do things to honor and thank them. Take a moment to bless your spouse or someone you love today.

But if serving the Lord seems undesirable to you, then choose for
yourselves this day whom you will serve, whether the gods your
ancestors served beyond the Euphrates,
or the gods of the Amorites, in whose land you are living.
But as for me and my household, we will serve the Lord.
Joshua 24:15

Not long ago I wrote about a major rocket attack that took place against our main base here in Baghdad. A total of seventeen large, explosive rockets screamed in from a launch point miles away from the base. Three Soldiers were killed, and over thirty others were wounded.

What made this attack particularly upsetting was some recent information was released and it confirmed that Iraqi Police were significantly involved in the attack. It is hard to go out and fight day after day in a foreign country for the primary benefit of people we don't know. It becomes much harder when we realize that some of those we are helping and working with have not only betrayed us, but participated physically in the attack.

Since the attack, a number of those police officers who took part have been arrested, and it seems as if most of those responsible have been caught. Although every organization has "bad" people, the level of corruption in the Iraqi government, and specifically the police, is extremely bad. There are strong influences from organizations and people to be disloyal to the Government of Iraq. In some cases money is paid to garner allegiance. Other times the safety of individuals or their families is what is held in the balance. It is not an easily resolved situation, and the choices can be difficult. The decisions can literally be life and death for some of the Iraqi men and women.

The reality is we have the same choice in our spiritual life. Every day we are challenged in different areas to choose the way of God or choose the wrong way. Make sure that you take a good account and choose wisely whom or what you will serve. Make your commitment, "As for me and my house we will serve the Lord."

Take a few minutes to review the devotions you read during this past week. Write down three key lessons you learned. What aspect of the week's devotions resonates most with you? (If you are participating as a group or family take time to discuss these key lessons.)

_____

_____

_____

_____

Were there any aspects of the devotions that you had trouble identifying with? (If you are participating as a group or family take time to discuss the troubling portions.)

_____

_____

_____

_____

Write down names of people you know who might be struggling with some of the points from the devotions. Take time to pray for each person. (If you are participating as a group, or family take time to pray for the people identified.)

_____

_____

_____

_____

What changes do you feel God is calling you to make after reading last week's devotions? (If you are participating as a group or family take time to discuss those desired changes.)

_____

_____

_____

_____

Think about a personal example in your life that demonstrates the truth of the devotions. (If you are participating as a group or family take time to share some of the stories with each other.)

_____

_____

_____

_____

Take delight in the Lord, and he will give you the desires of your heart. Commit your way to the Lord; trust in him and he will do this: He will make your righteous reward shine like the dawn, your vindication like the noonday sun.

Psalm 37:4-6

There is an old song that has a stanza that reads, *"He's got the whole world in His hands, He's got the whole world in His hands, He's got the whole world in His hands, He's got the whole world in His hands."* The wonderful implication is that God has control of the world, and that the world is not a burden for God. Additionally the lyrics indicate the world is something God can easily hold securely and even gently in His strong but compassionate hands.

The opposite view of this is perhaps best portrayed in the Greek mythology of Atlas. Atlas is best known from a sculpture that shows a wonderfully well-built and strong man. Despite all his muscles and his strength, he strains to hold the heavens on his shoulders, the punishment he has received from Zeus for leading the Titans in rebellion. Atlas is supposed to represent the most powerful of the Titans, but he can barely stand under his burden; in fact, he is unable to stand fully erect.

I thought about all this as we finished our conference in Bahrain. One of our presentations was about some of the efforts in the area of Africa. I listened with interest to all the sad problems, the tragic issues in Africa, and the myriad attempts to help the people who struggle with poverty, disease, and injustice. I firmly believe in the need for and responsibility of Christians reaching out to the poor, the hurt, the sick, and the oppressed. The caring hand of God is often extended as Christians reach out in obedience to the call to "love your neighbor." But, we can't do it in our own strength. We will only be like Atlas if we attempt to do it on our own. However, if we rely on God's strength and direction, committing ourselves and our actions to God and trusting God, we will find that the burden will be as easy as holding a light load in our hands.

The Lord reigns, he is robed in majesty; the Lord is robed in majesty and armed with strength; indeed, the world is established, firm and secure The seas have lifted up, Lord, the seas have lifted up their voice; the seas have lifted up their pounding waves. Mightier than the thunder of the great waters, mightier than the breakers of the sea—
the Lord on high is mighty.
Psalm 93: 1, 3-4

The earth trembles and our bodies shake as the powerful helicopters roar overhead. Whether it is simply lying on my bed inside my containerized housing unit (CHU), walking across our base camp, or out at a remote location with fighting Soldiers, there is a sound that brings a sense of awe and comfort. Because we control the skies, the sound of helicopters is a good thing to hear, even at those unexpected times when it jolts us from sleep or a conversation. Most of the time when we hear the helicopters, we know they are engaged in an important mission. They take Soldiers, Marines, and others in Iraq and Afghanistan from one place to another. In some of the areas of Afghanistan where our Soldiers carry out missions, it would be almost impossible to get there safely without helicopter support. Helicopters pick up our wounded Soldiers and quickly take them to our medical facilities. Helicopters also transport badly needed supplies to our personnel at remote locations. So, it is good to feel that rumbling and shaking caused by the low flying aircraft that thunder over our heads.

At one point in my military career, I was assigned to an infantry battalion with the Twenty-fifth Infantry Division in Hawaii. One of the things I enjoyed was going to the North shore area of Oahu when the big, gigantic waves were coming in. The power and might of those waves were evident, and the roar they created was awesome to hear.

The awesomeness of our helicopters reflects enormous power and might, but they pale in comparison to the power and majesty of God. Even the seas and their greatness are but a reflection of the true glory and majesty of God. We serve a great and mighty God who is worthy of our devotion and love.

Now I want you to know, brothers and sisters, that what has happened to me has actually served to advance the gospel. As a result, it has become clear throughout the whole palace guard and to everyone else that I am in chains for Christ. And because of my chains, most of the brothers and sisters have become confident in the Lord and dare all the more to proclaim the gospel without fear.
Philippians 1:12-14

What is your perspective during hard times? When you find yourself in periods that are difficult and when just surviving seems unimaginable, what is your attitude?

I found that some folks in Iraq and Afghanistan who are Christians often develop a not so healthy attitude or perspective during their time downrange. Obviously, being in combat, away from home, and in a strange country is difficult. Hard living conditions, the threat of death or serious injury from combat actions, and the loneliness of being separated from those they love contribute greatly to the mindset Soldiers sometimes develop. Some people cultivate the attitude of "just hanging on," and they take on a focus of just finishing the assignment. They fail to realize or take advantage of the great opportunity they have to reach out to others and to share God's love and peace.

The Scripture reading today gives us a good picture of the attitude God would like to see us display when we find ourselves in difficult circumstances. First, God is not surprised about any situation in which we end up. Being in Afghanistan, Iraq, jail, a hospital, a bad class at school, or even a difficult relationship, is not a surprise to God. That may not be what God wanted to see from you or others, but it is not a shock. As Paul writes in verse 12, God can use even the worst situation to advance the Good News.

Other points in this text that are important to understand are: We are called by Christ for a purpose, to be an encourager in the midst of difficulty, and to know that God will see us through.

Make sure your perspective is similar to what Paul records in our reading. Don't be short sighted or fail to see the impact you can have on others, especially during hard times.

Anyone who does not provide for their relatives, and especially for their own household, has denied the faith and is worse than an unbeliever.
1 Timothy 5:8

Happy Birthday! Happy Anniversary! Happy Day! Yesterday was my brother's birthday. I wish I were back in the United States and were able to be with him and maybe take him to dinner. Of course being here in Iraq makes getting together impossible, but I was able to call my brother a few days ago, speak with him, and wish him a Happy Birthday over the phone. I also sent him a birthday card to express my wishes for a Happy Birthday and to tell him I loved him.

It is easy to get caught up in our day-to-day activities of life and forget to affirm our love and affection for those we love the most. For Soldiers in Afghanistan and Iraq, the danger is focusing so much on the combat that we lose sight of the rest of our life. For you it might be making more sales, conducting an important business meeting, trying to get good grades at school, or training for an athletic event. None of those things are bad; in fact, they are very worthwhile endeavors. Yet, if they cause you not to uphold and show the appropriate love and care for family and other important people in your life, your priorities are out of balance. Providing for family and those you love demands more than just food and shelter. It calls for emotional and spiritual provision as well.

Some things are just wrong and have no place in our life. However, most activities have value or hold a needed place in our life. The key is to find the correct balance for each activity in our lives. Have you been devoting enough time and effort to those who need and deserve your attention? Take a moment today to focus on that part of your life.

My help comes from the Lord, the Maker of heaven and earth.
He will not let your foot slip—
he who watches over you will not slumber;
indeed, he who watches over Israel will neither slumber nor sleep.
Psalm 121:2-4

Some of the Soldiers here were talking about the extremely difficult terrain in the Northeast portion of Iraq, close to the border of Turkey. Much like a majority of the terrain in Afghanistan, it is a rugged, mountainous area. The slopes are steep and high, and the valleys are deep and hard to navigate. Those Soldiers were specifically talking about the rough paths that they had to travel in those mountain regions.

The discussion reminded me of when I was stationed in Colorado. Some friends and I used to regularly run on the trail that twisted and turned its way up Pikes Peak. This mountain stretches majestically over 14,000 feet high from its base. The run up the mountain, even only half-way, can be draining, but sometimes the run down is even harder on the legs and body. One time one of the guys running with us complained about all the rocks, bumps, and ruts. It was not uncommon when we were running hard down the side of the mountain to find ourselves tripping and falling because of a misstep caused by one of those bumps or ruts. Yet, the other amazing thing is that those same bumps, rocks, and ruts could also be used as great helps. As we ran up the mountain, they were actually what we pushed off against. Coming down the mountain, strategically using these obstacles kept us from losing complete control as our feet braced against the side of a bump, a rut, or a big solid rock.

Sometimes the difficulties God allows in our life can be used to help us, even though that might not seem like the initial intent. No matter what, know that God is with you all along the way.

Do not get drunk on wine, which leads to debauchery. Instead, be
filled with the Spirit, speaking to one another
with psalms, hymns, and songs from the Spirit.
Sing and make music from your heart to the Lord, always giving
thanks to God the Father for everything,
in the name of our Lord Jesus Christ.
Submit to one another out of reverence for Christ.
Ephesians 5:18-21

Humbleness, gentleness, and submissiveness are usually not the
normal words used to describe our best leaders in the Army. Yet, those
qualities should be clearly evident in our leaders who are Christians.
Men and women who are followers of Christ are not exempt from the
responsibility to be leaders who exhibit these qualities in their lives. We
are also called not to be the type of leader who throws his or her weight
around because of a position of authority.

There was a Brigade Commander, a full colonel in charge of a few
thousand Soldiers, he was also a committed Christian who had a long
distinguished career in the military. This man had been a staff officer at
the Pentagon, had commanded Soldiers at the company and battalion
level (and now a brigade in combat), and had also been a key planner
for the operations of one of our large formations of Soldiers from a
Division that carried out the first actions in Iraq. He was an important
man with lots of responsibility and authority.

This man was asked about his success and specifically why he was so
intent over the years to be a leader who was respectful of others but still
got things done effectively without being rude, over-bearing, or mean.
His reply was on target, "God calls me first to be a servant of His and
then a Soldier in the U.S. Army. The good thing is my being a Christian
makes me a better and more effective Soldier and leader," he stated.

Do you want to be the best leader or person you can be?
Incorporating the precepts of God in your life will make you better in
those elements of your life. Additionally, you'll know that you are being
faithful to the call of God in your life as well.

Be shepherds of God's flock that is under your care, watching over them—
not because you must, but because you are willing, as God wants you to be;
not pursuing dishonest gain, but eager to serve;
not lording it over those entrusted to you, but being examples to the
flock.
1 Peter 5: 2-3

As the commander of his own Brigade Combat Team (BCT), as well as the Forward Operating Base (FOB) that housed the BCT and some additional combat units, the hours seemed endless, and sleep was a precious commodity. There are no days off in combat, especially for the commander. However, the schedule, what we call the battle rhythm, was designed with a more relaxed pace on Sundays for the men and women on the FOB to "catch their breath" for just a short time if possible. Sometimes the battle rhythm worked, and sometimes the enemy placed a vote that forced us out of that plan.

As much as he wanted to sleep an extra hour or so on some Sundays, this commander faithfully got up and attended chapel services every Sunday. When I talked to him about leadership, he brought this up as an example. He said he knew that God would be okay with his taking a day every once in a while to sleep in or relax, but he also knew that his attendance on a regular basis was a strong example to the Soldiers and other leaders in his unit and on the FOB. He felt that Soldiers should take the time to worship in their tradition and faith.

The same principle of leading by example is seen in the business world, teaching young salesmen and women how to "seal a deal." It is seen when fathers and mothers show their sons and daughters how to catch and throw a ball or how to cope with disappointment. My mom taught me basic sewing skills and the importance of starting each day by making my bed, which helped instill a sense of discipline.

Leading by example is most importantly carried out in the arena of faith. Living a life of service and devotion to God and walking with God day to day is best seen in the life of faithful believers. You must be willing to live out the life you are trying to pass along to others - family, friends, co-workers, and neighbors.

Take a few minutes to review the devotions you read during this past week. Write down three key lessons you learned. What aspect of the week's devotions resonates most with you? (If you are participating as a group or family take time to discuss these key lessons.)

_____

_____

_____

_____

Were there any aspects of the devotions that you had trouble identifying with? (If you are participating as a group or family take time to discuss the troubling portions.)

_____

_____

_____

_____

Write down names of people you know who might be struggling with some of the points from the devotions. Take time to pray for each person. (If you are participating as a group, or family take time to pray for the people identified.)

_____

_____

_____

_____

What changes do you feel God is calling you to make after reading last week's devotions? (If you are participating as a group or family take time to discuss those desired changes.)

_____

_____

_____

_____

Think about a personal example in your life that demonstrates the truth of the devotions. (If you are participating as a group or family take time to share some of the stories with each other.)

_____

_____

_____

_____

They were helped in fighting them, and God delivered the Hagrites and all their allies into their hands, because they cried out to him during the battle. He answered their prayers, because they trusted in him.
1 Peter 5: 2-3

I had just finished an early morning run when I heard the distinct sound of an incoming rocket. I was outside the large concrete barriers that are set-up around all our containerized housing units (CHUs). I quickly moved inside the barrier wall and started to get down on the ground as loud explosions rattled the area.

Recently, we have seen big improvements in the overall security and a sharp drop in the attacks and violence in Iraq. However, the base where I live in Baghdad has increasingly come under indirect fire from rockets and mortars, even as other violence has decreased. The attack I described above consisted of about fifteen powerful rockets. Since then there have been several other similar attacks. During one of those attacks, where the rockets seemed to be landing right near my CHU, I found myself lying prostrate on the floor next to my little single bed.

As you might imagine, I say some well-focused and intentional prayers during those type of attacks. After lying on the floor for the duration of this recent series of rockets, I thought about how appropriate it is to have prayer at critical times. That should be the default action of Christians who come under attack in any form. The attacks could be physical, like rockets and mortars; or the attacks are more likely to be spiritual, emotional, relational, financial, or mental.

Such a default response has to be programmed in our lives through intentional, continual prayer. Unlike our computers, where we do a onetime program default, our prayer responses have to be reinforced by a regular program of coming to God and spending time talking with God and listening to God = Prayer.

I have no greater joy than to hear that my children
are walking in the truth.
3 John 1:4

You will know the truth and the truth will set you free.
John 8:32

Sometimes a great and powerful truth is right in front of us, but we fail or refuse to see the wonder of what could be. The following statements are humorous but also sad in their lack of vision.

"I think there is a world market for maybe five computers," Thomas Watson, Chairman of IBM, 1943. *"This 'telephone' has too many shortcomings to be seriously considered as a means of communication. The device is inherently of no value to us,"* Western Union internal memo, 1876. *"The wireless music box has no imaginable commercial value. Who would pay for a message sent to nobody in particular?"* David Sarnoff's associates in response to his urgings for investment in the radio in the 1920s. *"We don't like their sound, and guitar music is on the way out,"* Decca Recording Company rejecting the Beatles in 1962. *"Heavier-than-air flying machines are impossible,"* Lord Kelven, president, Royal Society, 1895. *"Louis Pasteur's theory of germs is ridiculous fiction,"* Pierre Pachet, professor at Toulouse, 1872. *"There is no reason anyone would want a computer in their home,"* Ken Olson, president of Digital Equipment Corporation, 1977.

Many people do the same thing with Jesus, as the folks did with their opportunities, as seen in the quotes above. The truth was standing right in front of them offering them freedom and strength, but they refused to see it. Do you have a vision for the truth? Don't be scared to step forward with God. It may seem like folly, but it is not.

Have I not commanded you? Be strong and courageous. Do not be afraid; do not be discouraged, for the Lord your God will be with you wherever you go.
Joshua 1:9

What is courage? I once read a quote by John Wayne that said something to the effect that courage is mounting up on your horse and going out to face the enemy despite your fears. Every day our Soldiers, Sailors, Airmen, and Marines display this type of amazing courage. As they go out the gate of our bases, they know that the enemy has set ambushes using the methods of improvised explosive devices, snipers, suicide bombers, and other types of explosive weapons in order to kill or wound them. Yet, time and time again those troops do exactly what Wayne was getting at in his definition of courage. Despite the fear they may feel, they "mount up" and go out to face vicious threats.

When I was assigned to the 82nd Airborne Division, I used to parachute from planes and jets. Sometimes my wife and daughter would come out to the drop zone and watch me and the other Soldiers as we parachuted from high above. My daughter was only about four years old at this time, and this was her only real experience with planes and flying. When we moved to our new assignment in Hawaii, we had to fly. As we got closer to the destination, she started to cry. When I asked her why she was crying, she replied that she was scared. "Why are you scared," I asked? She replied in her little four-year old voice, "I've never parachuted from a plane and it scares me, but I'll jump!" Now that is courage.

Courage is not the absence of fear, but the act of taking the right action despite your fear. Is there something you have been avoiding due to fear? God calls us to be courageous men and women. You can trust in God and give your fears over to God. Be courageous and act today.

Therefore do not worry about tomorrow,
for tomorrow will worry about itself.
Each day has enough trouble of its own.
Matthew 6:34

Yesterday, the devotion was about courage. I purposely wrote about the amazing courage our Soldiers, Sailors, Airmen, and Marines demonstrate every day. But courage does not equate with a lack of worry.

A young Soldier who works in our office had started to impress me. Each day I come into the office after my early morning run. Often I'm the first one in, and no one shows up until after I leave for an early morning meeting at the headquarters led by Lieutenant General Odierno and General Petrateus. Lately, this Soldier had been coming in shortly after me and working hard getting the office ready for the day. A couple times he even beat me into the office. I complimented him about his hard work and his commitment to the mission.

His work and effort were good, but I found out yesterday that he was coming into work because he could not sleep due to worry. The recent rocket attacks had him a little frazzled and focused on possible injury or death.

Many of the things most of us worry about never happen. When at times our worries do come to fruition, the grace of God is always enough to see us through. I admit I am guilty of spending a sleepless night or fretting away hours of precious time due to worry or anxiety. However, I know such worry is a non-productive endeavor for anyone, but especially for Christians. This does not mean we should not spend time planning and thinking through the possible pros and cons of future actions. It certainly does not mean we should not spend time in prayer seeking the wisdom and guidance of God for decisions in our life. God wants us to use wisdom in our actions, but we need not fret about life. Lay down the worries of your life at the feet of God.

The brothers and sisters there had heard that we were coming,
and they traveled as far as the Forum of Appius
and the Three Taverns to meet us.
At the sight of these people Paul thanked God and was encouraged.
Acts 28:15

A small group of U.S. Soldiers was attacked by a large group of enemy insurgents. For a short period of time, it seemed as if the Soldiers, who were pinned down by the enemy fire, might not be able to maneuver to defeat the enemy or get to safety. Then a supporting unit of Soldiers arrived and drove the enemy away. The young officer who was leading the first group talked about his feelings and thoughts when he saw the Soldiers appear on the scene. "I thanked God for their arrival and was encouraged about our predicament," he said.

Today's Scripture reminded me of an experience I once had while climbing Mount Saint Helens. A friend and I had camped overnight at the trail head so we could get a good early start up the mountain. We had waited a long time to get our climbing permit and could hardly wait to begin. The next morning dawned with a beautiful sunrise and we began our trek to the top of this still active volcano. When we were about three quarters of the way up, we came across a lone individual. He had grown tired and slowed the progress of his climbing party. His group had left him there and told him they'd pick him up on their way down. My friend asked him if he wanted to go up with us. I was apprehensive, not wanting to slow our climb up the mountain. My friend encouraged him, and he agreed to climb with us. All three of us made it to the top, and what a glorious view and fantastic accomplishment it turned out to be.

The arrival and subsequent encouragement from others is just what many people need to help them through a hard time. You can and should be one of those who uplifts others. Wherever you go, make it your mission to arrive and find a way to be an encourager to those you encounter.

I say to myself, "The Lord is my portion;
therefore I will wait for him."
Lamentations 3:24

The Soldier was hunched over in his seat. His hands held his head as he sobbed, overcome by sorrow and pain. He and about two hundred other Soldiers were at a small, sparse, makeshift chapel at a Forward Operating Base in Baqubah, Iraq. A Memorial Ceremony to honor and remember three of his fellow Soldiers who were killed in action a few days earlier was just finishing. Numerous other Soldiers, including myself, were wiping the tears from our eyes. The loss and tragedy that war brings creates many appropriate times for shedding tears of sorrow and loss. It makes many folks question the involvement in combat. Often there is a lack of vision, and understanding that the temptation to do nothing and to allow evil or injustice to remain can bring even more tears in the long run.

Jeremiah wrote the book of Lamentations. His life experiences, and the suffering he witnessed Israel endure, caused him to be a man who wept. He recorded the captivity of Judah, the destruction of Jerusalem, and the horrid condition of people he loved. Yet, in the midst of all this, Jeremiah wrote the words we read today, "The Lord is my portion; therefore I will wait for Him." Another version I once read says, "The Lord is my portion; therefore I will hope in Him."

All of us, Christians included, face sorrow, devastating loss, and heartache at some point or points in our lives. These are times when tears are normal and expected. Tears shed in such circumstances don't indicate a lack of faith or trust in God, rather they are signs of normalcy in a fallen world. The lives of Jeremiah and Jesus tell us we don't need to exhibit a false joy when weeping or sorrow is the norm. Rest assured that tears are often appropriate. Take heart that times of sorrow can lead to renewal and joy if you allow God to be a part of your heartache.

Command them to do good, to be rich in good deeds,
and to be generous and willing to share.
1 Timothy 6:18

The vehicle was overflowing with boxes of items designated for Soldiers, Sailors, Airmen, and Marines assigned to duty in Iraq for up to fifteen months. Those boxes had been picked up at the postal detachment on base and were being taken to the chaplain offices to be recorded, sorted, and then distributed to the men and women serving our nation in this place far from home.

The outpouring of concern demonstrated in the giving of items for Soldiers, as well as thousands of items for an outreach program we conduct called, "Hearts for Baghdad," is phenomenal. The latter program provides clothing, general medical supplies, hygiene items, and baby products to Iraqi families that are struggling to survive in their war-torn country. The willingness of people in the United States to give to people in Iraq they don't know is truly touching.

The giving is not limited to the folks back in America sending goods to Iraq. Some of the most wonderful projects are those planned and conducted by U.S. Soldiers that are here in Iraq. These men and women, who at any time are at high risk of injury or death, nevertheless take their time and resources to reach out to the Iraqi people. Numerous school projects have been conducted. Those projects built or repaired school buildings and provided school supplies. Other programs include helping orphanages, sponsoring a nursing school, repairing and cleaning local homes and shops, and distributing sports equipment and playground items to Iraqi children.

God wants us to be a giving and caring people who reach out in the loving name of Jesus to a hurting, needy world. Find a place, a group, or even a single person that needs some help, and find a way to reach out and assist today.

Take a few minutes to review the devotions you read during this past week. Write down three key lessons you learned. What aspect of the week's devotions resonates most with you? (If you are participating as a group or family take time to discuss these key lessons.)

_____

_____

_____

_____

Were there any aspects of the devotions that you had trouble identifying with? (If you are participating as a group or family take time to discuss the troubling portions.)

_____

_____

_____

_____

Write down names of people you know who might be struggling with some of the points from the devotions. Take time to pray for each person. (If you are participating as a group, or family take time to pray for the people identified.)

_____

_____

_____

_____

What changes do you feel God is calling you to make after reading last week's devotions? (If you are participating as a group or family take time to discuss those desired changes.)

_____

_____

_____

_____

Think about a personal example in your life that demonstrates the truth of the devotions. (If you are participating as a group or family take time to share some of the stories with each other.)

_____

_____

_____

_____

Because of the Lord's great love we are not consumed, for his
compassions never fail. They are new every morning;
great is your faithfulness.
Lamentations 3:22-23

A few days ago the devotional Scripture was from chapter 3, verse 24 of the book of Lamentations. Just prior to that Scripture verse are today's two deeply meaningful verses. Remember that the writer, Jeremiah, has been subjected to seeing terrible events that caused him to weep. The Temple, built by Solomon, was not only a magnificent and beautiful architectural structure, but it was also the dwelling place of God for the people of Israel. The temple was the heart of Israel's corporate lives. Not only was the Temple destroyed when the Babylonians invaded Jerusalem, but the brutal invasion left Jerusalem and the country in ruins. Sickness, slavery, starvation, and suffering were the norm at this point in the lives of most of the people of Israel.

Here in Iraq I have been blessed to visit the ruins of Saint Elijah's Monastery near the city of Mosul. It is a fourth to fifth century monastery complex that houses a wonderfully ancient Christian sanctuary. It is the oldest Christian church in Iraq.

I have also visited the ruins at the Old Testament city of Ur in the Tallil area. This once beautiful city that sat next to the Euphrates River was the home of Abraham (Abram), and the ziggurat there is still mostly standing, thanks to a restoration project.

The destruction and loss of these amazing places and the current level of destruction and violence in Iraq and Afghanistan are sad events. From ancient times till today, the world has always known destruction. Today, there is sense of excitement and thankfulness as the situation in Iraq appears to get better. Regardless of the good or bad that has happened, is happening, or will happen, the lesson today and always is the eternal faithfulness and compassion of God. Trust in God!

Praise be to the God and Father of our Lord Jesus Christ,
the Father of compassion and the God of all comfort, who comforts
us in all our troubles, so that we can comfort those in any trouble
with the comfort we ourselves receive from God.
2 Corinthians 1:3-4

The hardest and worst part of being assigned to a combat zone is seeing and dealing with the death of Soldiers, Sailors, Airmen, and Marines. When a Soldier is killed in Baghdad, Mosul, Ramadi, Kandahar, Kabul, Jalalabad, or any of the other areas in which we operate in Iraq and Afghanistan, numerous people are impacted by the death.

Families are the first folks we think of as being effected by a Soldier death. Everyone grieves differently when they suffer a loss and helping them can be difficult. One of the most effective means of helping seems to be the reaching out and the care offered by those who have previously had a spouse or child killed in combat. Gold Star is an organization that is made up of women and men who have lost spouse or child to war. Their basic mission is to provide a safe place and an understanding presence for a current parent or spouse who has suffered the death of a loved one. They offer a shared experience that provides a deeper insight about the feelings associated with losing a loved one in combat. Amazingly, many of those people being cared for eventually become one of those providing care.

The same thing happens with the Soldiers themselves. Those who have previously had a close friend and fellow Soldier killed in combat are able to help those Soldiers who are going through such deaths in the present. Then later, those Soldiers will offer their understanding to another hurting warrior.

God knows the need for and the importance of comfort for the hurting, and God provides for that comfort. The Lord often calls those people who have experienced pain, loss and grief to be used as God's hands to help others. You too can be God's instrument of peace and comfort. Determine how you might help someone who is struggling in life or experiencing the pain of loss.

No discipline seems pleasant at the time, but painful.
Later on, however, it produces a harvest of righteousness
and peace for those who have been trained by it.
Hebrews 12:11

Living and fighting in Iraq and Afghanistan, or living, working, or going to school in New York City, Cleveland, Washington D.C., Atlanta, Dallas, Phoenix, San Francisco, Boston, Miami, St. Louis, Chicago, Seattle, Los Angeles, or any location in the world can be hard. There are always difficult circumstances that are ahead, no matter where we are. But can good come from the hard times? Can pain bring joy? The answer is yes. If we have the attitude and determination that we will allow God to bring growth in any situation, then indeed good can come from bad and light can shine in the midst of darkness.

It often seems that when someone's life is going through a rough period she or he has a greater tendency to seek out God and search for God's direction. David echoes that experience when he writes about God in Psalm 119. He writes, "It is good that I was experiencing hard times because I learned of your guidance."

I often see senior sergeants "getting on" to our young Soldiers. Sometimes this chastening seems harsh, and I'm sure it is a painful experience for the younger Soldier. However, the result is most often a better trained and better prepared Soldier.

If we are willing to listen and learn, allowing God to teach us in the midst of our pain and hardship, it can make us better men and women. It can also serve to make us better Christians, and draw us closer to God. It is not so much what happens in life, but how you react to what happens that is important.

If you find yourself in the midst of difficult circumstances, ask God to use those difficulties in your life to help you grow in wisdom and strength. You may find that as you look back on your life, it was in the times of trial and hardship when you bloomed the most.

Jesus asked, "Were not all ten cleansed? Where are the other nine?
Luke 17:17

As I write this, Thanksgiving Day is upon us, and even in Iraq we are looking forward to celebrating in our own special way. At home, in the United States, one of the hallmarks of this holiday is the gathering of family and close friends for a big delicious meal. The people who gather may also watch a parade, and will most likely spend time watching TV and cheering on a favorite football team. Then there are the specific family food traditions of turkey, dressing, gravy, cranberries, macaroni and cheese, sweet potato pie, green bean casserole, cheeses, pumpkin pie, pecan pie, chocolate pie, apple pie, and lots of other goodies.

The Soldiers, Sailors, Airmen, and Marines who are downrange will also come together in locations throughout Afghanistan and Iraq. Our spouses, children, brothers, sisters, parents, and other family members can't gather around the table with us, but we will have a family celebration. The groups that sit down at a big military dining facility or a makeshift table at a security point in Baghdad are part of a family that has been forged in sweat, blood, and shared hardship. There is a thankfulness and deep sense of gratitude to be with one another on this day. At all those places we will give thanks for our comrades who have died or been wounded so seriously that they can't be with us. We will not forget them. An empty place at a table will be set for those missing warriors. The empty seat and unused setting is to remind us of their sacrifice on our behalf.

Today's Scripture verse looks at an event where nine of ten people forgot or chose not to give thanks for their specific blessing. Often we are not much different than those nine. We quickly forget to thank others and especially God.

I want to encourage you not to take for granted the blessings and favor of God in your life. Make sure you are the one who returns and gives thanks to God.

I have no one else like him,
who will show genuine concern for your welfare.
Philippians 2:20

I spoke with one of our Soldiers yesterday who is going through a difficult time. In the course of our conversation, he said he knew that I would care enough to listen and actually pray for his situation. He also told me about someone who noticed he was a little down, and offered him some caring words from the heart. There are, for all of us, those times when we need someone to care for us.

The story is told of the day that Albert Schweitzer, the great medical missionary, philosopher, theologian, and physician, was arriving by train in New York City. Dr. Schweitzer was coming to New York to receive a prestigious award. As he got off the train at Union Station, he was greeted by a large crowd that included many dignitaries and several church leaders. As he drew near to the crowd, several people came forward to carry his two bags and a case. There were also some reporters there who wanted to interview this amazing man. Everyone was vying for his attention.

As he stood there, Dr. Schweitzer noticed an old black woman struggling with her one bag and using a walking cane as she attempted to make her way slowly across the terminal. The great man excused himself, walked through the crowd, and approached the woman. He took her bag, helped her out the door, hailed a cab, and pre-paid her fare.

That woman needed a little loving kindness and concern, and Dr. Schweitzer was the instrument God used, primarily because he had made himself aware and available. Is God trying to use you? Are you listening to His call to care for others? You can make a difference in the life of another person. Show God's care to someone today.

There is a way that appears to be right,
but in the end it leads to death.
Proverbs 14:12

The man looked like any other Iraqi who was at the open market. The sky was a clear brilliant blue. The sun was out, but the temperature was gloriously comfortable. Young children were enjoying running from shop to shop and looking at the birds, food items, and other goods on sale. The parents walked casually behind, keeping a close eye on their children, but enjoying the time out. For the first time in a long time, Baghdad did not seem to be under siege from al-Qaeda or other insurgents. The market and many shops had re-opened, and numerous people were taking advantage of that welcome change.

Without warning the market area was ripped apart by a crazed insurgent wearing a suicide vest. The man who had seemed to be just one of the crowd was wearing an explosive suicide vest under his robe. The explosion caused numerous deaths and scores of injuries, many to young children. I wondered, as the chaotic reports came in, what would make a man with supposed religious motivation from his Muslim faith think that an action like this would somehow be pleasing or acceptable to God.

Of course, purposely taking innocent life is not acceptable or pleasing to God. The man was deluded in his faith. He had been convinced or had convinced himself that he was somehow right in his heinous actions. Sadly, what he believed to be right resulted not only in his physical death, but also his spiritual death, separated from God for eternity. Only a commitment to Jesus will prevent us from not ending up in the same place.

A new command I give you: Love one another.
As I have loved you, so you must love one another.
John 13:34

Last night over four hundred Soldiers, Sailors, Airmen, Marines, and civilian employees assigned to the Camp Victory and Camp Liberty, Iraq complex attended a Christmas Eve Candlelight Service. The service was held in the rotunda of the Al-Faw Palace. This beautiful building was one of the many palaces that Saadam built throughout Iraq. The headquarters for Multi-National Corp-Iraq is now located inside the palace; therefore, we decided to use this magnificent structure for the Christmas Eve service. It seemed more than a little ironic to be celebrating the birth of Jesus in this place that was built by such an evil person, who is on the opposite end of the spectrum from Jesus.

What a glorious and joyful service it was! We read Bible passages that helped us remember and focus on the events leading to Jesus' birth. We sang a number of Christmas hymns and had a wonderful time of prayer. Additionally, we had special music by a contemporary Christian group named "Joyful Noez" and also by the Camp Victory Gospel Choir, comprised mostly of Black Soldiers. Both groups brought their own unique, but beautiful style of worship to the service. It was a wonderful blessing to be a part of a service that lifted up Jesus in such a different place, with such a diverse group.

What a sharp contrast to what had gone on in that palace before and what was going on around us on the streets of Baghdad. It was a marvelous night of praise, worship, and fellowship.

Love one another and let your light shine in the midst of darkness!

Take a few minutes to review the devotions you read during this past week. Write down three key lessons you learned. What aspect of the week's devotions resonates most with you? (If you are participating as a group or family take time to discuss these key lessons.)

_____

_____

_____

_____

Were there any aspects of the devotions that you had trouble identifying with? (If you are participating as a group or family take time to discuss the troubling portions.)

_____

_____

_____

_____

Write down names of people you know who might be struggling with some of the points from the devotions. Take time to pray for each person. (If you are participating as a group, or family take time to pray for the people identified.)

_____

_____

_____

_____

What changes do you feel God is calling you to make after reading last week's devotions? (If you are participating as a group or family take time to discuss those desired changes.)

_____

_____

_____

_____

Think about a personal example in your life that demonstrates the truth of the devotions. (If you are participating as a group or family take time to share some of the stories with each other.)

_____

_____

_____

_____